HOW TO DRIVE A
STEAM LOCOMOTIVE

Brian Hollingsworth

ASTRAGAL BOOKS · LONDON

Forward tears along in the moonlight, distant signal showing clear (*Ink and wash drawing by George Heiron*)

First published in 1979 by Astragal Books, an imprint of The Architectural Press Limited, London

Reprinted 1983, 1987

© Brian Hollingsworth 1979

Designed by Cluny Gillies
Printed and bound in Great Britain by Mackays of Chatham Limited

CONTENTS

ACKNOWLEDGEMENTS

The author's thanks are due to Alexandra Artley for thinking of the idea and to her colleague Lindsay Miller for seeing the book through to the press stage; to John Wilks, orchestra conductor and locomotive builder extraordinary, for suggesting who might write it. Equally helpful have been people connected with the Festiniog Railway—Allan Garraway, the General Manager, who made time at the busiest period of the year to read the manuscript through and make valuable suggestions; Seamus Rogers, volunteer engineman, for writing an excellent account of his experiences. A very special sort of gratitude is owed to Jane Lewis, who turned spidery heiroglyphics into a respectable manuscript.

As regards the pictures, the author would like to thank especially Emery Gulash of Detroit, Bob Jones of London, David Scudamore of Northampton and Patrick Whitehouse of Birmingham for being exceptionally forthcoming and helpful in meeting the requirements.

The effect of too low a water level (*British Rail*)

The boiler of this engine exploded, in Glo'ster Station yard, close to the water tank, on February 7th, 1855.

INTRODUCTION

Once upon a time, according to tradition, the dearest ambition of every small boy was to become an engine driver; implying, of course, that the sort of engine meant was a Steam Railway Express Locomotive. Alas, throughout the span of living memory, railways have been steadily descending from being the sole means of mechanical land transport to mere co-existence with motor cars, lorries and aircraft. For this reason engine driving jobs have been hard to come by and the road from engine-cleaner to fireman to shunting-engine driver and eventually to main line express driver very long. Indeed, many good men were still waiting for promotion—by seniority—to the 'top link', as it was called, when retirement overtook them. Apart from around the end of World War II, when quite young men could find themselves drivers, the ladder to taking charge of a steam express was very difficult to get on to and took an exeedingly long time to climb. In recent times, therefore, small boys had to be content with careers leading to less attractive positions, such as prime ministers, industrial tycoons or field marshals.

Since 1945, it has not so much been the world's railways which have been declining, but their use of steam power. From some 250,000 steam locomotives operational then, numbers have come down to a mere 25,000 now, as this book is begun. When it comes to be published, the total will be significantly less, for the fires are being finally drawn, not by ones and twos, but dozens at a time, as diesels and electrics take over. It is hard also to imagine any development of the energy situation in which the mechanically simple but greedy-of-fuel steam engine will make a serious come-back as an instrument of commerce.

It is sad enough that such a marvellous creation as the steam locomotive should vanish, but sadder still that the skills and knowledge that made it possible should disappear also. It is just 150 years since George and Robert Stephenson's *Rocket* beat all comers at the locomotive trials at Rainhill on the first inter-city railway in the world, that from Liverpool to Manchester. The Stephensons were not by any means the first to put a locomotive on rails—that honour went thirty years before to a Cornishman called Richard Trevithick. Neither was *Rocket* by any means their first locomotive. What is remarkable about her is that 150 years later, when only one nation in

The British school of design: an LNER K4 2–6–0 (*Rodney Wildsmith*)

The American school of design: a Chicago, Burlington & Quincy 4–8–4 (*Brian Hollingsworth*)

The Japanese took their locomotive practice direct from the United States: a D51 Mikado near Tokyo (*Brian Hollingsworth*)

the world is still building steam locomotives for other than pleasure use, the principles on which they are constructed are identical to those of *Rocket*. During those 150 years, many attempts were made to improve the steam locomotive by changing the principles of design, but none prevailed. It was refinement rather than change which succeeded.

In this process of refinement, there were two main schools. These were, respectively, the American and the British. The thinking of these two very different schools permeates railways in every corner of the globe and the dream journeys of the first part of this book reflect this. An attempt has been made to cover both American and British practice and, in particular, to highlight the contrasts between them. It is interesting that the Japanese, in many ways now the world leaders of the art, in their imitative days took their locomotive practice direct from the United States and their signalling and operating from Britain.

There arises also that difference between American and British terminology. Should we speak of cars, trucks and stacks; or coaches, bogies and chimneys? In the event, whichever term sounds or suits best has been used; the context being relied on to resolve any ambiguity.

Nearly fifty years ago, when he was at the impressionable age of seven, a beloved aunt gave the writer a book called *The Dreamland Express,* written and illustrated by H.R. Millar. It has remained one of his favourites ever since. It described how three boys dreamt, as we are going to do, that they took charge of a giant steam locomotive—'a superheated Baltic and oil-fired too'. The book's perfection was marred by one shortcoming and it was this, that 'there must have been some magic about that engine, because exactly at the moment when the boys' feet touched the footplate, they found they knew all about it'. To my mind half the fun is finding out about driving a steam locomotive and, of course, that is the intention of this book.

The hazards encountered by the young engineman on H. R. Millar's *Dreamland Express* were a little out of the ordinary, but not absolutely unknown on the world's railways (*H. R. Millar*)

Centenarian *Dolgoch* heads up the Talyllyn Railway, Merioneth (*Talyllyn Railway*)

The first task for the dreamers is to tackle a real section of railway with a dream locomotive; this is a dream in both senses: the loco never existed (though it could have) and it also would have had few rivals for ease of working. The general style of design is American and the locomotive is based on the only steam locos still in production in the world today, but with oil firing and many other conveniences. The railway is Brunel's famous main line through Cornwall and Devon; its steep gradients, twists and turns, plus the heavy trains made working on it exacting for the drivers. Oil firing did come briefly just after World War II—the writer's first solo

Camilla Hollingsworth takes charge of 2–8–2 *Queen of Colorado* (*Brian Hollingsworth*)

Facing page:
0–6–2T No. 5 backs down on to her train at Grosmont, North Yorkshire Moors Railway (*Author's collection*)

5

assignment as an engineering pupil on the Great Western Railway was to design the oil fuel depôts there. In contrast to this ride on a steam locomotive of the 1970s, there is a brief interlude concerned with one of the 1840s.

The second task is to tackle a dream railroad with a real locomotive. The real locomotive is one of special personal interest to the writer—he was instrumental in rescuing it from the scrap-man's torch when British Rail gave up steam ten years ago. He also—it can now be told—drove it himself over British Rail lines on several occasions. And could one possibly site a dream railroad (assuming it had to be American) anywhere else but in the State of Colorado, 'garden of the gods'?

In this way something is told of the wide range of steam locomotive work which once existed. The book goes on to talk about 'how to drive a steam locomotive' in the sense of 'how to get to drive one today'. Opportunities on tourist lines, in working museums and on railways in miniature are discussed. Then we come to the considerable 'live steam' movement, made up of those who build and run their

own steam locomotives, mainly clubbing together to do it. Lastly and in conclusion, imagination is resorted to once more in some thoughts on the chances of an oil-less Britain once more putting her trust in steam—describing what it might look like and where it might operate should such an unlikely event ever happen.

Railway and steam have played a large part in my life and brought me more pleasure than I can conveniently describe. It is my hope that through this book I can share some of it with you.

Penrhyndeudraeth
1978

Brian Hollingsworth

The Hussar does the knots
on the 5 in. gauge—on the
track of the Peterborough
Society of Model Engineers
(*Bob Jones*)

PART ONE:

THE DREAM

K.C. Jones was the engineer's name,
   On a six-eight-wheeler he won his fame,
Looked at his watch an' his watch was slow,
   Looked at the water an' the water was low,
Put in yo' water, an' shovel in yo' coal,
   Stick yo' head out the winda, watch them drivers roll,
And the switchmen knew by the engine's moans
That the man at the throttle was Casey Jones.

                    American railroad song—Anon

FORWARD

One night I dreamt that Steam was back and that you, reader, and I were invited to take charge of a mighty locomotive on a long, fast and important train. In my dream I knew it was no reincarnated museum-piece or pleasure line machine, but instead just a well-maintained working locomotive doing the job it was built to do. The first thing we did was to climb high above the rails up a metal ladder into the cab; the second was to contemplate with awe the sixty or so handles, levers and wheels that form the controls. The surprising thing is that the actual driving of this huge machine, if it is in good order and not over-loaded, is easier than driving the ordinary small car, which may have only one-fifth the number of controls. It could be said it is like driving a car without having to steer or change gear.

Problems of driving
It is not how to drive the locomotive that presents the problems; at least, not in the narrow sense. It is driving in the wider sense—including keeping steam up and running the train—that has all the difficulties and hazards. These are such that no sensible person who owns or has steam engines, be they 530-ton 'Big Boys' or 10lb methylated spirit toys, ever lets anyone whose experience is at all in doubt take charge of one. That is why our adventure must be the stuff that dreams are made on.

The controls
Penrhyndeudraeth is a real Welsh mouthful, but taken by syllables (*Pen* = headland, *rhyn* = between, *deu* = two, *draeth* = beaches) the full meaning becomes clear.

The controls in this cab of ours respond to the same treatment. First, there are those which merely turn things on and would normally stay in that position all the time the locomotive is in action. A prime example is the valve that turns on the steam to the pump that supplies compressed air. Once turned on, an automatic governor valve looks after things. A second category includes those for dealing with extraneous things like steam for heating the train, whilst a third lot are provided to cover rare emergencies. This is another reason why locomotive driving is restricted to people who have done a lot of it; knowing what to do in a situation that occurs only once in a hundred runs is something that is not acquired quickly. Dismissing

Previous pages:
Steam engines, be they 530 ton 'Big Boys' or toys, should never be handled by the inexperienced (*Union Pacific Railroad Museum Collection*)

The first thing we did was to climb high above the rails up a metal ladder into the cab (*Brian Hollingsworth*)

all these controls—Figure 1 shows which they are—the dozen that are left present an altogether less awesome aspect. And these in their turn divide six-by-six into fireman's controls and driver's controls—combustion and traction, if you like. The key to Fig 1 lists the controls divided into the categories just described above.

Fundamental principles

It seemed sensible even in the dream to say a word first on the fundamental principles by which this beloved Iron Horse works and moves. The most fundamental one of all is that unconfined steam takes up 1325 times as much room as the water from which it came; confine it—in a cylinder with a piston, say—and the steam will push. Therefore, by addding levers and wheels, steam can be made to move things. Remember how, long ago, a certain James Watt watched a kettle boiling on the hob with its lid rattling and saw then that this was how to harness the power of steam; hence, mechanical transport by land and sea and—to quote the plaque on the wall of the original station at Stockton, County Durham—thereby 'marking an epoch in the history of mankind'.

The boiler

Thus the two main elements of a steam locomotive are respectively the kettle part, known as the boiler and which produces the steam; and the mechanism which turns the steam into work, known often as the engine part. The boiler is the most striking feature of a locomotive and as its workings are both hazardous and unfamiliar it comes first in our consideration. Just inside the boiler at the back where we are standing and very obvious to us by its heat and humming is a furnace—in our case an oil-fired one—contained in a box, the firebox, in fact. The firebox is closed on all sides except the bottom in order to separate the water from the fire. It is absolutely crucial that the water level in the boiler is never allowed to fall below

An awesome sight: the sixty or so handles, levers and wheels that form the controls (*North-West Museum of Science and Industry*)

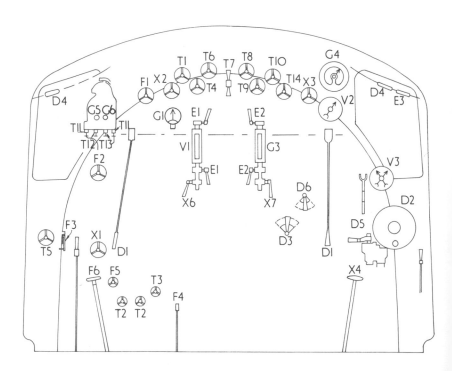

1 *Forward*'s controls

Key to Diagram

Driver's main running controls (see Chapter 3)
The driver works with these six controls
D1 Regulator or throttle (with left-hand and right-hand handles)
D2 Reversing wheel
D3 Cylinder cock operating lever
D4 Whistle cord (regular whistle)
D5 Air brake valve
D6 Sanding control

Fireman's main running controls (see Chapter 2)
F1 Steam valve for exhaust steam injector
F2 Blower
F3 Oil fuel control or latch
F4 Damper lever
F5 Oil fuel atomiser control valve
F6 Water valve for exhaust steam injector

Emergency controls
E1 Water-gauge isolation cocks, left-hand (2)
E2 Water-gauge isolation cocks, right-hand (2)
E3 Whistle cord (emergency whistle) left-hand and right-hand

Vital gauges
V1 Boiler water-level gauge (the most vital of all)
V2 Pressure of steam in the boiler
V3 Pressures of air in the brake system (a duplex gauge showing air pressures in the brake pipe and in the main reservoir)

At this we can draw the line between vital and merely important controls

'Turn-on' controls
The controls in this category are the ones which normally do not need any adjustment during a run.
T1 Oil burning steam supply
T2 Steam to clear fuel lines (2)
T3 Steam to heat oil fuel in cold weather
T4 Steam to oil manifold
T5 Steam to oil manifold from external supply

T6 Turn on turbo-generator to supply current for electric lights
T7 Main shut-off valve for all auxiliaries
T8 Steam for atomising cylinder lubricating oil
T9 Steam to air-compressor
T10 Steam to air compressor lubricator
T11 Air compressor lubricator drain
T12 Air compressor lubricator feed valve I
T13 Air compressor lubricator feed valve II
T14 Steam to cylinder cocks
(Electric light switches (12)—not shown)

Occasional controls
Some valves and controls are only used or adjusted occasionally on the run.
X1 Inlet valve for external steam supply (used when raising steam)
X2 Steam supply to the train for heating
X3 Steam valve for live-steam injector
X4 Water valve for live-steam injector
X5 Water control for exhaust steam injector
X6 Water gauge blow-down (for cleaning glass), left-hand
X7 Ditto, right-hand
(Cancellation handle for Automatic Warning System apparatus—not shown)

Gauges
Next are listed the significant (but not vital) gauges, sight glasses etc.
G1 Pressure of steam in train heating pipe
G2 Pressure of steam supplied for atomising oil fuel
G3 Second boiler water gauge
G4 Speedometer
G5 Air compressor lubricator—sight feed No. 1
G6 Air compressor lubricator—sight feed No. 2

Tender controls and gauges
Hand-brake handle
Water scoop handle
Fuel contents gauge
Water contents gauge

(These are not shown on the diagram, being situated at the front of the tender, but of course are accessible to the crew)

the top plate of the firebox. This thought is one that must never leave you when in charge of a steam boiler and applies equally to all sizes from 10 ft diameter down to 2 in.

Tubes lead the hot gases from the fire forward through the boiler to the smoke-box at the front and so up the chimney, heating the water in the process. The level of this water is revealed to us by the meniscus, bobbing up and down in those little glass tubes. The sight of them is a constantly sought comfort, because when the level can be

As of 1978, the only steam
locomotive type in the world
still in production: a
Chinese *Forward* class
2–10–2 (*Dave Scudamore*)

A handsome brass plate on
the smoke deflector plate—
naming locomotives is very
much a British custom
(*Rodney Wildsmith*)

seen it is neither too high or too low. Too high a water level puts
water instead of steam into the mechanism of the locomotive with
dire result and the effect of too low a level is comparable to boiling a
kettle dry—in the same way that a world war is comparable to a
boxing match. Without doubt the water gauge is the most important
of the nine gauges provided in this cab.

A rather desperate last ditch safety measure against the con-
sequences of too low a water level uncovering the firebox crown are
the so-called lead plugs screwed into it. These are actually brass
plugs with a lead core. Should they become overheated the lead core
will melt and a surge of steam will—to some extent—smother the fire.
Alas, such measures have not, over the years, entirely prevented
occasional disastrous boiler explosions on locomotives whilst in the
hands of inexpert or careless crews.

Supporting the boiler system are three feed arrangements, two (one
in reserve) for replenishing the boiler, ie, by injecting water into it,
and one to spray atomised oil into the firebox. The tanks in the
tender, as well as the pipes and valves which comprise these
arrangements, are the fireman's direct concern and their detailed
operation is described in Chapter 2.

Also under the fireman's direction is the water scoop for filling the
tender tank on the run, from troughs set between the rails. The
arrangements for supplying steam for heating the train are also his
worry. Steam is also used to generate compressed air for braking and
sanding, electric current for lighting and a force for working the
reversing gear on the locomotive. Hydraulic pressure accumulated
by a hand pump is used for the locking mechanism of the reversing
gear.

Coat of Arms of the Great
Central Railway

Forward

The engine part of the locomotive is best observed from the ground; ours makes a fine sight standing amid the yard lights, finished in green with a handsome brass plate on the smoke deflector plates displaying the name *Forward*. Naming locomotives is a British custom, but the name is *Forward's* only British feature, as she is basically American in design and concept, first passing from America to Russia and thence to China.

The name salutes the Great Central Railway Company, whose motto it was when in the 1890s they built England's last main line from near Nottingham to Marylebone Station, London. It also honours the last steam locomotive in the world to remain in production, the QJ or *Forward* Class of the Chinese National Railways, to which ours bears a marked resemblance. At Tatung works, north-west of Peking, QJs were still being built as late as 1978. Like the QJs, ours is what is called a 2–10–2; the 10 in the middle signifies five pairs of coupled driving wheels, enough to give ample traction on the hills which lie ahead. The 2s at either end signify single pairs of small guiding wheels mounted in what are called pony trucks. Diagramatically a 2–10–2 could be shown so . . . oOOOOOo; in America the type is called Santa Fé after the railroad which introduced it. The use of ten coupled wheels for passenger traffic is not common, but it occurred on some lines, notably on the Canadian Pacific where there were oil-fired *Selkirk* type 2–10–4s (oOOOOOoo); British Rail ran class 9 2–10–0s (oOOOOO) on passenger work occasionally.

More common for passenger traffic were *Northerns* or 4–8–4s (ooOOOOoo), *Pacifics* or 4–6–2s (ooOOOo). *Ten-wheelers* or 4–6–0s (ooOOO), 4–4–0s (ooOO), 4–2–2s (ooOo) and 2–2–2s (oOo) take us back

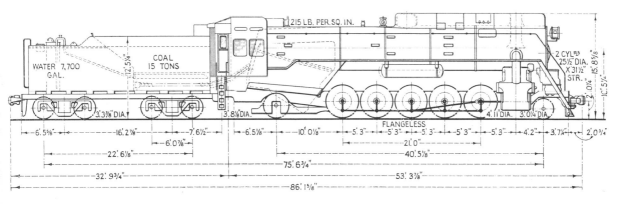

2 Diagram of *Forward* showing principal weights and dimensions (Note: this diagram shows a coal-burning locomotive, not oil-burning as described in the text) (*Railway Gazette International*)

Heating surface, tubes
  large and small 2560 sq ft
  firebox 270 ft
Total evaporative 2830 sq ft

Superheater 1549 sq ft
Combined heating surface 4379 sq ft
Grate area 73.2 sq ft

Weight (in working order)
  engine 133 tons
  plus tender 217 tons
Weight on coupled wheels 100 tons
Tractive effort 63,000 lbs

through time to Stephenson's *Rocket,* which was an 0–2–2 (Oo). H.R. Millar's *Baltic* meant it was a 4–6–4 (ooOOOoo), known in America as *Hudson.*

Our dream *Forward* differs from the Chinese ones by being oil-fired, instead of mechanically stoked with coal and also by being for passenger as well as freight service. Her dimensions are shown in Fig 2.

The mechanism

As on 99% of the steam locomotives built during the last fifty years—most of the exceptions were in Britain and France—virtually all *Forward*'s mechanical works are outside in full view. Steam pressure is converted into mechanical force by the pistons which slide to and fro in the cylinders. Unlike the working of a petrol engine, the pressure can be applied on both sides of the piston and hence the force has to be transmitted to the outside world via a (hopefully) steam-tight gland through which the piston rod moves. At the end of the piston rod is fixed the crosshead and to the cross-head is pinned—with a pin of 5 in. diameter—the little end of the connecting rod. The other end, the 'big-end', works on an even bigger $8\frac{1}{2}$ in. pin, fixed off centre to the third coupled wheel, as you can clearly see in Fig 3. Pushing on the piston turns first this wheel and then, via a set of what are called coupling rods (very obvious), the others.

You might think there is a problem when the piston is at one end of its travel, with the connecting rod in line with the piston rod and hence having no leverage—what is called 'dead centre'. But go round

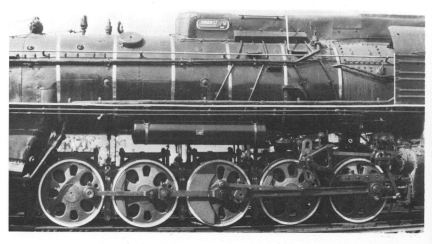

3   Piston valve
SC Steam chest
E   Exhaust chamber
SP Steam port
P   Piston head

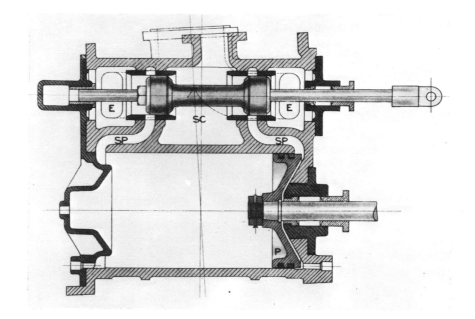

to the other side and the motion there will be found to be in one of the best possible positions, being set at 90° to this side.

The simplicity of the steam engine is seen very clearly displayed. A diesel of equivalent power will have, hidden away in its much more complex innards, maybe 32 cylinders and connecting rods. That bland exterior hides a maze of complications . . .

A pair of smaller pistons—piston-valves—on the upper spindle entering the cylinders, control the admission of steam and its subsequent exhaust up the chimney. If you push the spindle forwards, that is, away from the cab, openings (ports) are uncovered so that steam is admitted at the front end of the cylinder, that is, the end away from the cab, which forces the piston backwards. As our locomotive is standing, with the rods at the bottom position, the backwards push will result in the wheels trying to turn anti-clockwise and, hence, forward movement. If the rods are at the top position, the valve spindle has to be moved backwards to get forward motion. On the other hand if, with the rods down, the valve spindle is moved backwards, then things are the other way round and the locomotive will try and move in reverse. At the same time these valves open other ports so that the steam can get out of the cylinder after it has done its work.

A linkage of smaller rods called the valve gear achieves these movements. The valve gear that *Forward* and virtually all other modern steam locomotives have is called Walschaerts, after the Belgian who invented it in 1856, but never lived to see its general adoption in the 1900s.

Walschaerts gear, Fig 4, is very simple and so arranged that what is called a return crank pin oscillates the valve rod. When the crank is in the bottom position the valve rod is fully forward, so forward motion is achieved. If reverse is desired the valve rod can be moved in

17

Walschaerts Valve Gear in fore gear: rods down, valve forward, steam admitted in front of the piston. The wheels try to turn anticlockwise and the loco moves forward (*Brian Hollingsworth*)

Walschaerts Valve Gear in fore gear: rods up, valve backward, steam admitted behind the piston. The wheels try to turn anticlockwise and the loco moves forward (*Brian Hollingsworth*)

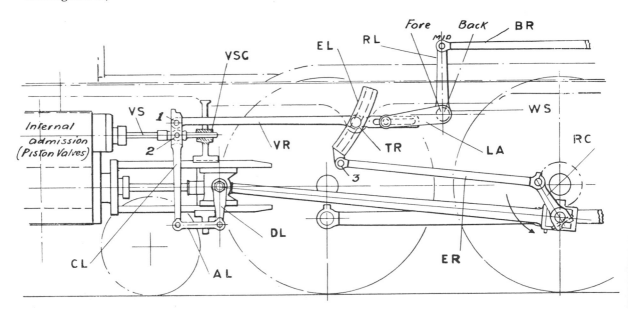

4 Walschaert's valve gear (Author's collection)
Joint 1 Valve rod to combination lever
Joint 2 Combination lever to valve spindle
Joint 3 Eccentric rod to expansion link

AL Anchor link	LA Lifting arm	
BR Bridle rod	RC Return crank	
CL Combination lever	TR Expansion link trunnion	
DL Drop link	VR Valve or radius rod	
EL Expansion link	VS Valve spindle	
ER Eccentric rod	VSG Valve-spindle guide	

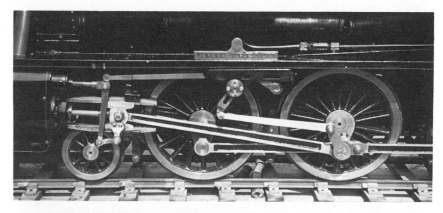

Walschaerts Valve Gear in back gear: rods down, valve back, steam admitted behind the piston. The wheels try to turn clockwise and the loco moves backwards (*Brian Hollingsworth*)

Walschaerts Valve Gear in back gear: rods up, valve forwards, steam admitted in front of piston. The wheels try to turn clockwise and the loco moves backwards (*Brian Hollingsworth*)

a link to the opposite side of a pivot, as regards its connection to the return crank. This reverses the motion and, since, in the 'rods down' position, the valve spindle is moved backwards, backwards movement ensues.

There is also a secondary linkage up near the cylinders, whose main component is called the combination lever. This is in connection with a mystery known as 'lap and lead', which basically involves biasing the opening of the valve towards the early part of the stroke, rather than exactly half-way as it would otherwise have been.

The brakes

In spite of its name, *Forward* is also able to stop, using the crude but effective method of pressing those cast-iron brake blocks against the wheels. The force to do this is provided through a fairly complex linkage by air pressure in a cylinder—with yet another piston—controlled from the cab. Out on the line it is the train rather than the locomotive which does the stopping; the train brakes are called the 'automatic air brake' and will be considered when we are connected up to one. For the locomotive on its own a simpler brake called the 'straight' air brake is provided. There is also a hand-brake—used as a parking brake except in dire emergency—which works on the tender wheels.

2

HOW'S THE WATER?

THE FIREMAN'S DUTIES

Injectors

It has been said that the most vital question to ask on a steam locomotive is the one posed by the title of this chapter. And if the answer is unsatisfactory, steps have to be taken to put more water into the boiler. This is done with an injector, of which our locomotive has two, fitted one on each side under the cab. An injector is an arrangement of cones inside a metal casing, whereby water from the tender tank is introduced into a steam jet, mixed with it in what is called the combining cone and squirted through a feed pipe and non-return valves (known as clack valves) into the boiler. It was an invention, dating from the 1850s, of a Frenchman called Henri Giffard, who actually intended it for a steam driven aircraft. This early spin-off from the space age soon replaced, on the majority of steam locomotives, the complex and troublesome mechanical feed-pumps which previously had to be used.

The injector, Fig 5, is a delightful device (and Monsieur Giffard a very ingenious fellow), because in spite of its simplicity and lack of moving parts, it seems to do what is obviously impossible, ie, to force water into the boiler against pressure which must be greater than that of the steam the device is supplied with. There is an air of magic—something for nothing, if you like—about the injector, in spite of the fact that in one's head one knows that it must obey the laws of nature like everything else.

The sleight-of-hand which deceives us lies in the way in which an injector converts pressure into movement and vice versa. Steam entering the device at the end flows into the cone, **1**, fixed wide end first. Like a river entering narrows, the speed of the steam flow increases and it shoots out of the nozzle at high speed. This first cone is called the steam cone.

The second cone, **2**, is called the mixing or combining cone and is again fixed wide-end first. Water is introduced into the gap between the two cones and it becomes mixed with the steam jet issuing from the first cone. This steam condenses in the water, imparting its velocity to the mixture, the result being a high speed jet of water coming out of the nozzle of the second or combining cone.

The third or delivery cone, **3,** is fixed the opposite way round, nozzle end first. The high-speed water jet is squirted *into* this nozzle—it has a

The placing of an injector in relation to the cab (*Brian Hollingsworth*)

Close-up of a live steam injector (*Brian Hollingsworth*)

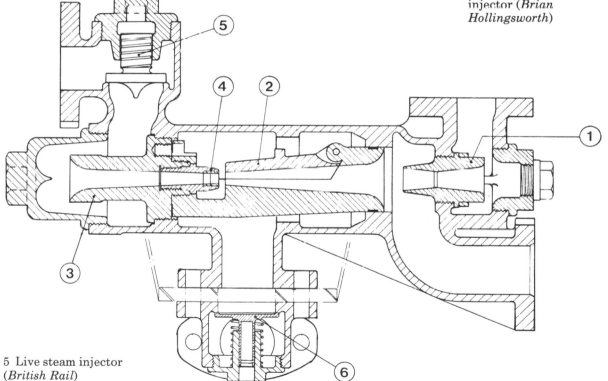

5 Live steam injector (*British Rail*)

lip, **4**, formed round it for this reason. In this cone, speed is traded for pressure as the water proceeds along to the wide end. Now a jet of water is different to a jet of steam—it is much heavier for one thing and, for another, it is incompressible—and sufficient pressure and, hence, force is developed to open, against boiler pressure, the non-return valve, **5**, on the boiler feed pipe. In this way water is fed into the boiler; the rate of feed can be adjusted by the setting of the water control.

The basic *modus operandi* is to open the injector water valve first, then open the steam. If all is correct, the injector will pick up with a satisfying singing noise, the sweetest tune that any engineman can hear. The steam and water valve openings have to be adjusted correctly relative to one another for a particular pressure; otherwise water or steam streams from the overflow pipe conveniently placed for observation under the cab side. On this luxury machine, an electric light assists our view of it in the dark. There is naturally a non-return valve on this overflow pipe, **6**, to allow water or steam to escape but not permit air to be drawn in.

Problems arise with an injector when the cones either become worn or become coated with dirt or scale; or when there is an air leak into the water supply pipe; or when that pipe is obstructed. Valves may not be seating properly or the feed water may be too hot for the steam to condense into. Some of these defects may make the injector work only intermittently or only at certain pressures. Hopefully neither of ours will be like this, as nothing is more distracting when running a steam locomotive than an injector upon which one cannot rely. Recalcitrant injectors can often be taught manners by fiddling with the valves. Opening the steam valve very quickly, for example, or, perhaps, opening it very slowly. Waiting a while after opening the water valve is another trick that may make a temperamental injector see sense.

Exhaust steam injector

Actually our injectors are not alike; the one on the right is as has been described. The one on the left has even more sleight-of-hand about it. It is called an exhaust injector, Figs 6 and 7, because it uses the low pressure steam exhausted from the cylinders—at 10 lb per sq. in, say—to squirt water into the boiler at 225 lb. It is true that the exhaust steam is augmented by a supplementary supply of live steam but even so it is a remarkable conjuring trick in the application of natural laws.

6 Exhaust steam injector

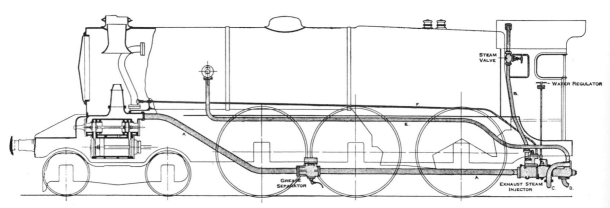

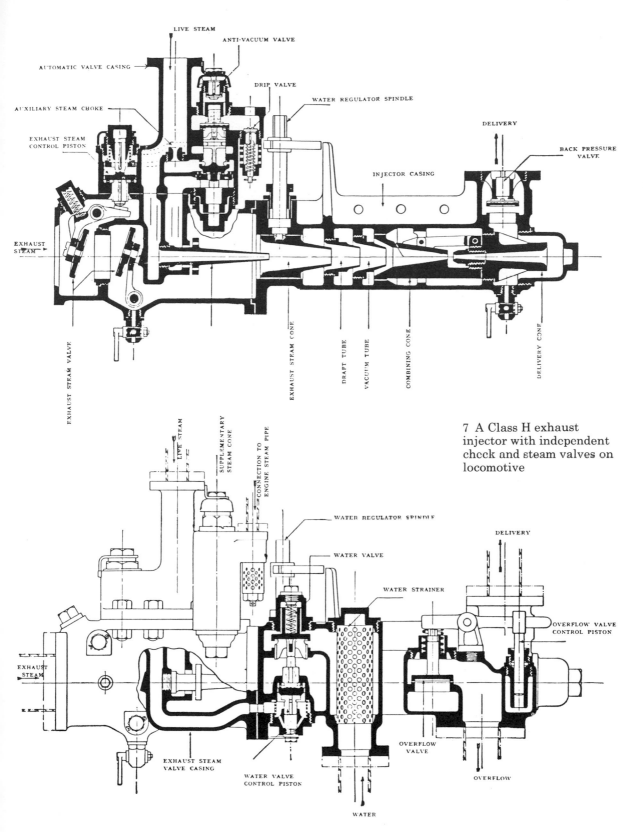

LIVE STEAM

ANTI-VACUUM VALVE

AUTOMATIC VALVE CASING

DRIP VALVE

WATER REGULATOR SPINDLE

AUXILIARY STEAM CHOKE

DELIVERY

BACK PRESSURE VALVE

EXHAUST STEAM CONTROL PISTON

INJECTOR CASING

EXHAUST STEAM

EXHAUST STEAM VALVE

EXHAUST STEAM CONE

DRAFT TUBE

VACUUM TUBE

COMBINING CONE

DELIVERY CONE

7 A Class H exhaust injector with independent check and steam valves on locomotive

LIVE STEAM

SUPPLEMENTARY STEAM CONE

CONNECTION TO ENGINE STEAM PIPE

WATER REGULATOR SPINDLE

WATER VALVE

DELIVERY

WATER STRAINER

OVERFLOW VALVE CONTROL PISTON

EXHAUST STEAM

EXHAUST STEAM VALVE CASING

WATER VALVE CONTROL PISTON

OVERFLOW VALVE

OVERFLOW

WATER

23

In spite of (or perhaps because of) being a more complicated piece of apparatus, the exhaust injector is even easier to operate than the live steam one. The water valve can be opened and left, then the steam valve is opened whenever the injector is required to operate. An automatic valve switches off the water whenever the steam is shut off. If exhaust steam pressure is available, i.e. the locomotive is running with the steam on, the injector will use it. If not, there is another automatic valve which changes its working over to 100% live steam. Of course, the point of using exhaust steam for feeding the boiler is the considerable saving in steam and, hence, fuel that results; about one gallon (or one shovelful of coal) in sixteen is usual.

Forgive me for having dealt at such length with what must seem to you to be a mere piece of plumbing. However, as we go on I hope you will come to realise that no more crucial or important equipment exists on a steam locomotive.

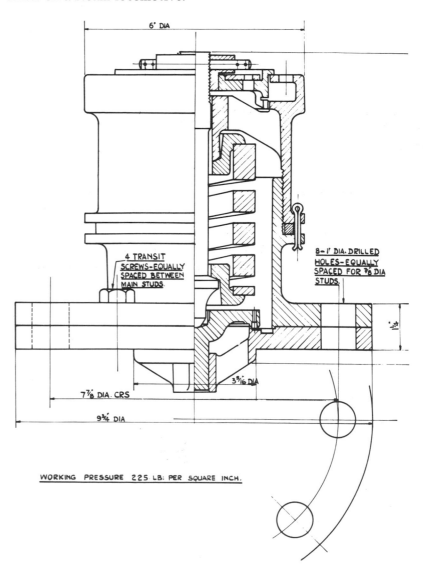

8 Ross pop type safety valve (*North West Museum of Science and Industry*)

Three safety valves stand on the sky-line of the boiler (*North-West Museum of Science and Industry*)

Pressure gauge and safety valves

The next question that a fireman has to worry about is 'How's the steam?' The answer is given partly by that clock-like thing called a boiler pressure gauge (see **VI**, Fig 1). This currently records 160 lb per sq. in., well below the red mark on the gauge at 225. Should pressure rise above the red mark, there is a danger of over-stressing (and in the limit exploding) the boiler. To prevent this happening, safety valves (see Fig 8) are provided in the top of the boiler . . . there they are just in front of the cab. By the time 226 lb per sq. in. is reached, one or more will open with a violent pop and deafening roar.

Oil burners

We've an oil-burner tonight and accordingly can turn up the wick as we wish. If it had been a coal burner there would be questions of building up the fire, removing clinkers or ash and other laborious matters. A look through the peep-hole in the firebox door shows us the smallest of flames emanating from the backwards-facing burner low down at the front of the firebox. Enough heat is being supplied just to keep her warm and run the auxiliaries; perhaps one gallon of oil per minute is being burnt, whereas wide-open the same burner can burn oil at seven times that rate.

To 'turn up the wick' is not just a question of opening up the oil valve (see **F3**, Fig 1) usually called the oil latch; to burn the oil we need more air. Although it is not quite so critical, more steam to vaporise the additional oil will be needed as well. The valve which controls the amount of draught when the locomotive is stationary is called the blower (see **F2**, Fig 1). This valve sends a jet of steam up the chimney (smoke stack), causing a draught through the tubes and hence drawing air into the firebox, through air spaces below. The size of these air spaces can be altered by the damper lever (see **F4**, Fig 1).

So, to change our fire from a candle-flame into a raging furnace, both blower and oil latch have to be opened in step, with an occasional adjustment of the atomising steam valve (see **F5**, Fig 1) to match. One can see if blower and latch are correct in relation to each other by looking at the colour of the smoke issuing from the chimney. First, switch on the chimney light to see what we are doing. If the smoke is black, there is too much oil; adjust accordingly. The best conditions occur when there is a light brown haze at the chimney top.

25

When running, the amount of air drawn into the firebox depends on the draw of the blast up the chimney, which in its turn depends on the amount of steam being used. So, whenever the throttle is opened and the engine begins to pull, you have to follow this movement with the oil latch or firing handle, already referred to (see **F3**, Fig 1); similarly whenever the throttle is closed. Of course, this suits the boiler's need—when the throttle is opened more steam is used, therefore more fuel needs to be burnt to keep things on the boil.

The amount of air can also be regulated at this end by opening or shutting a damper (see **F4**, Fig 1) or air-door below the firebox. For a particular loco there is usually a fixed setting that is found to keep steam production in line with the amount used.

Steam heat

During all but the summer months, a fireman on passenger work has to see to the provision of steam heat for the train. A valve and gauge (see **X2, G1** in Fig 1) are provided and, when the loco is connected to a train, should be adjusted to give 40–80 lb per sq. in., as laid down according to the number of carriages to be heated.

The tender

The tender is almost entirely the fireman's kingdom and there are gauges to be found showing the amount of water and oil present in their respective tanks. There are two large hand-wheels, one of which applies the hand-brake and the other raises and lowers a scoop so that we can fill up with water from troughs or pans between the rails while on the fly. 7,000 gallons of water and 2,500 gallons of oil are carried in the tender when full; but in our journey of approximately 200 miles we shall consume 12,500 gallons of water, whilst the oil will easily last us through. Hence the need to pick up water during the journey.

Lines of promotion

In the Anglo-Saxon tradition of enginemanship, being fireman is a step on the road to becoming a driver. In fact the two jobs are very different—the skills which the fireman needs in order to maintain steam are quite different to those which the driver needs to run a train satisfactorily. French railways recognized this by putting *chauffeurs* into a quite different line of promotiom to the drivers, who were called *mechaniciens,* an indication that they were trained as fitters in the shops. The official American title 'engineer' for the man who drives did not however indicate such an origin but then neither did the unofficial term 'hogger' imply any serving of time as a pig-farmer. Nevertheless the fact remains that the driver's skill is mainly directed to matters outside the locomotive—knowledge of rules, signals and the road ahead—while the fireman provides the brains and brawn to keep it moving.

3

FIRST REVOLUTIONS

THE DRIVER'S DUTIES

The regulator

Having got this boiler adequately full of water heated well above its natural boiling point and hence trying to expand itself 1,325 times, we must think about how to apply and control this powder-keg of energy. The main instrument is the number one control, the regulator or throttle (see **D1,** Fig 1), which opens and shuts an opening to a pipe leading from a boiler to the cylinders. When the regulator is opened, steam in the boiler has a chance to expand; hence pressure is applied to the pistons and, hence again, the locomotive is moved.

Reversing screw

The number two control is the reversing screw (see **D2,** Fig 1)— sometimes a reversing lever—which manipulates that arrangement of rods called a valve gear via a steam servo-mechanism. If this case it is the one known as the Hadfield Power Reverse. One winds the screw clockwise or forwards for running forward and anti-clockwise or backwards for running backward. Very simple, yes, but there is a complication. It is called cut-off; wind the handle as far as it will go either way—what is called full gear—and steam admission to the

The Hadfield Power Reverse (*North-West Museum of Science and Industry*)

A typical locomotive shed
scene: the Great Western
Railway at Didcot (*John
Ransom*)

A bishop oils round—the
late *Eric Treacy* (*Rodney
Wildsmith*)

cylinder is cut off when the piston is about three quarters or 75% of the way along. Such a late cut-off is necessary for starting but, since there is no provision for the steam to expand very much before it is exhausted at the end of the stroke, it is also very wasteful. So, for running, the cut-off point is brought forward by winding the reversing lever away from the full gear position. For fast running, an early cut-off of, say, 20% or 15% of the stroke will be used. A convenient neutral position in the centre, half-way between full forward and full reverse gear, is obligatory when a locomotive is left unattended for any reason. The geometry of the valve gear is arranged so as to achieve all this.

Cylinder cocks

One other lever needs to be used to start—that one down there opens what are called the cylinder cocks (see **D3,** Fig 1). When steam first enters cold cylinders it turns back to water. If the cylinder cocks (which are just openings) are left shut, the water will be unable to escape and as the piston reaches the end of its travel, the cylinder will be burst; the result a £20,000 repair job and, doubtless, unkind remarks on the driver's service record. And there is no safety catch— one just has to know and *always* remember. These particular ones are steam-operated, with an element of fail-safe, in that they are shut by turning steam on.

Starting

Though they are more concerned with stopping than starting it does of course help to release the brakes, although once moving the driver keeps his hand always within close reach of their conveniently placed handles. But braking is almost a subject of its own. One other handle (see **D6**, Fig 1) is provided to help starting, by means of which *sand* can be dropped on the rails to give the wheels a grip. It is also a rule on most railways before setting a locomotive into motion, to tug the *whistle cord* (see **D4,** Fig 1) and give a short blast as a warning.

Just to get the feel, let's try moving her up and down this siding. The cylinder cocks should have been left open, but first we check that the lever is in the open position. Next, wind the reverse lever (in our case actually a screw) into full forward gear, that is as far forward as it will go. Now the moment comes and when you do it for the first time it is indeed one to remember. First give the whistle cord a tug . . . whooo! The throttle on this engine moves fore and aft (others move sideways or up and down), there it is just above the seat. A firm pull should just ease it open—you don't need much steam to move slowly on the level without a train.

Our lady begins to roll with chuffing from the open cylinder cocks, and a kind of metallic rumbling sound; this is quite normal, nothing is wrong—remember, the tyres are made of steel rather than rubber. Now we have gone nearly far enough, so close the throttle and let her roll to a stand. Nothing to it, is there . . . try taking her back by yourself.

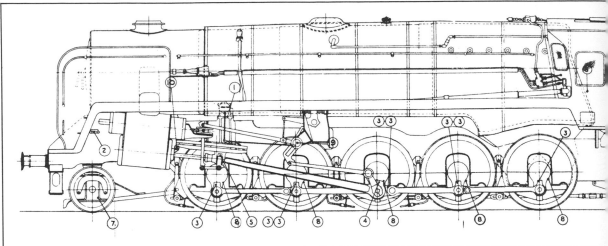

IDENTITY NO	TYPE OF LUBRICATOR	PARTS LUBRICATED	NUMBER OF LUBRICATORS.	
			L.H. SIDE.	R.H. SIDE.
I	MECHANICAL LUBRICATOR.	CYLINDERS.	1	—
		ENGINE.	—	1
2	OIL BOX.	PONY TRUCK CENTRE SLIDES & CENTRE.	2	3
3	OIL BOX & HOLE. (PART OF COUPLING ROD)	COUPLING RODS.	8	8
4	OIL BOX. (PART OF CONNECTING ROD)	BIG END JOURNALS.	1	1
5	OIL BOX. (PART OF CROSSHEAD ARM)	LITTLE END BEARINGS.	1	1
6	OIL SUMP.	REVERSING GEAR IN CAB.	1	—
7	OIL SUMP.	PONY TRUCK AXLEBOXES.	1	1
8	OIL SUMP.	COUPLED WHEEL AXLEBOXES.	5	5
9	OIL RECESS.	EXPANSION LINK DIE BLOCK	1	1
10	OIL BOX.	PISTON ROD SWAB CASE.	1	1
13	OIL FEEDER.	TENDER BRAKE BEVEL GEARS.	—	1
14	HOLE IN TENDER FRONT PLATE.	TENDER BRAKE SCREWS.	—	1
15	OIL FEEDER.	WATER PICK UP BEVEL GEARS. (WHERE FITTED)	1	—
16	HOLE IN TENDER FRONT PLATE.	WATER PICK UP SCREWS. (WHERE FITTED)	1	—
17	OIL SUMP.	TENDER ROLLER BEARING AXLEBOXES	3	3

9 Oil lubrication chart for
a 2–10–0 standard tender
engine, Class 9

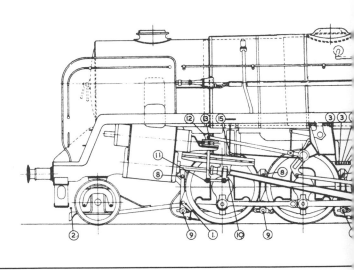

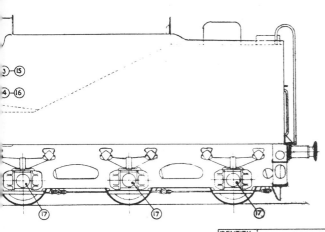

10 Grease lubrication chart for a 2–10–0 standard tender engine, Class 9

IDENTITY No.	DESCRIPTION	POSITION OF NIPPLES	No. OF POINTS	
			L.H.	R.H.
1	PONY TRUCK PIVOT	TOP OF PIVOT CENTRE PIN		1
2	PONY TRUCK AXLEBOX GUIDES	ON PONY TRUCK FRAME CROSS-STAY	2	2
3	COUPLED WHEEL AXLEBOX GUIDES	ON FRAME AT DRIVING WHEELS	10	10
4	BRAKE SHAFT BEARINGS (LEADING)	ON FRAME AT DRIVING WHEELS	1	1
5	BRAKE SHAFT BEARINGS (TRAILING)	ON FRONT OF REAR BUFFER BEAM.	1	1
6	FRONT FIREBOX SUPPORT SLIDES	ON SIDE OF ASHPAN	1	1
7	REAR FIREBOX SUPPORT SLIDES	ON SIDE OF ASHPAN.	1	1
8	BRAKE HANGER PIN	TOP OF BRAKE HANGER	5	5
9	BRAKE HANGER BOTTOM	BACK OF BRAKE HANGER	5	5
10	CROSSHEAD ARM TO UNION LINK	ON CROSSHEAD ARM	1	1
11	COMBINATION LEVER TO UNION LINK.	ON COMBINATION LEVER (BOTTOM)	1	1
12	COMBINATION LEVER TO P.V. CROSSHEAD	ON COMBINATION LEVER (TOP)	1	1
13	COMBINATION LEVER TO RADIUS ROD	ON COMBINATION LEVER (TOP)	1	1
14	RETURN CRANK ROD ROLLER BEARING	ON BEARING COVER PLATE	1	1
15	RATCHET LEVER TO DRIVING ROD	BOTTOM OF RATCHET LEVER	1	1
16	REGULATOR INTERMEDIATE LEVER	ON FRONT OF LEVER	1	–
17	REGULATOR HANDLE	ON HANDLE BOSS	1	1
18	DAMPER OPERATING SCREW & TRUNNIONS	ON DAMPER CONTROL COLUMN	–	4
19	ROCKING GRATE OPERATING LEVER.	ON LEVER BOSS	1	1

IDENTITY No.	DESCRIPTION	POSITION OF NIPPLES	No. OF POINTS	
			L.H.	R.H.
28	TENDER BRAKE SCREW	ON TENDER FRONT PLATE	–	3
29	TENDER BRAKE SHAFT TRUNNIONS	ON FRAME BEHIND FOOTSTEP.	–	2
30	TENDER AXLEBOX SPRING PAD	OUTER EDGE OF PAD	3	3
31	TENDER AXLEBOX GUIDES	BACK OF GUIDE FACE	6	6
32	TENDER BRAKE HANGER PIN	OUTSIDE FRAME ON HANGER PIN	3	3
33	TENDER BRAKE HANGER BOTTOM	BACK OF HANGER	3	3
FOR ENGINES FITTED WITH WATER PICK-UP GEAR				
41	WATER PICK-UP SCREW	ON TENDER FRONT PLATE	3	–
42	WATER PICK-UP SHAFT TRUNNIONS	ON FRAME BEHIND FOOTSTEP	2	–
43	HIND SHAFT WATER PICK-UP GEAR	ON FRAME BET INT & TRL.WHEELS	1	1
44	WATER PICK-UP SCOOP PIN	– DO –	–	1
45	WATER PICK-UP DEFLECTOR TRUNNIONS	– DO –	1	1

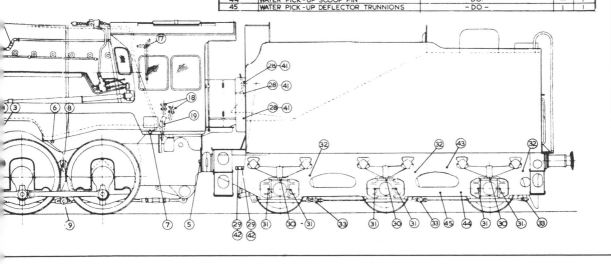

HOT BOX

Given by holding nose with fingers.

Places to oil—note mechanical lubricators on running board (*Rodney Wildsmith*)

Preparation

However, before we can make any serious moves with the engine, there are some very tedious but rather important matters to see to. A driver, as captain of the ship, has not only his own duties to perform but is also responsible for checking that the locomotive is in good working order. For example he should see both injectors tested and himself test the brakes and sanding gear. It is also the driver's job to go right round the engine in a systematic way, putting oil or grease on bearings, filling lubricators, and at the same time keeping a weather eye for any defects. If he needs to go between the wheels or put his arm inside the motion, safety must be considered by putting the engine in mid-gear (the steam equivalent of neutral in a motor-car), the hand-brake hard on and the cylinder cocks open. These three things are standard procedure in any situation vulnerable to involuntary movement of the locomotive. Another example would occur should we have to use the turntable in order to reverse direction or, indeed, at any time when there is no one on the footplate.

Oiling round

Lubrication of the locomotive is not only important but it is also complicated, (see Figs 9 and 10). For one thing, a bearing, slide or cylinder can be lubricated in one (occasionally more than one) of seven different ways. Even when a similar method is used, one place might require a different oil from another. On ours (as on the majority of modern steam locomotives), the cylinders and main axlebox bearings have top-class treatment with mechanical oil-pumps feeding oil through separate pipes to the parts to be lubricated. They are grouped in two reservoirs (those box-like things on the running plate) which have to be filled respectively with thick black treacly cylinder oil and for the axleboxes, thinner general purpose oil.

Another system is called displacement lubrication. There is one on *Forward* to lubricate the steam-driven air compressors. A trickle of steam is fed into an enclosed reservoir filled with cylinder oil. The steam condenses and turns to water. Since the water is heavier than the oil, the latter is displaced upwards by the former and so, rises above the exit pipe near the top of the reservoir. Thence it is carried down to the compressor's steam cylinders. To fill, shut off the steam supply, open the valve to drain condensed water from the reservoir, undo the filler cap (but remember, it will be hot) and fill with cylinder oil. There are two other separate valves to regulate the flow of oil, which can be observed in a rather fascinating way through glass tubes as drops of oil ascend in quick or slow succession, according to the rate of feed on their way to the cylinders.

Bearings and slides lubricated by syphon effect come next. These have a little reservoir to fill with oil and the only problem is knowing where they are so as not to leave any out. The feed is either through a wick known as a worsted tail trimming or worsted pad. The old school of drivers made their own but, like convenience foods, in the later years of steam such things would be drawn from the locomotive equivalent of the super-market, the stores. So important are the axle

Cylinders and valve-motion inside: an LNER *Claud Hamilton* 4–4–0 at Liverpool Street station (*Author's collection*)

Cylinders inside, valve-motion outside: Italian 640-class 2–6–0 (*Brian Hollingsworth*)

bearings that ours have both belt and braces in the form of pad lubrication as well as mechanical.

Worsted trimmings twisted up in a slightly different way are used as plugs to restrict the feed in pipes which lead oil by gravity or centrifugal force to places where it is needed. Instead of worsted plugs, needles or other metal restrictors can be used. The all-important bearings on our main rods are of this pattern.

Other bearings, especially roller- and ball-bearings, are lubricated by the familiar means of a grease gun applied to nipples. A quite different method of grease lubrication is used to the main rod bearings of some North American locomotives. Here, a cartridge of solid grease is put in the appropriate hole, arranged so that the grease stick is applied to the journal by light spring pressure.

Cylinders outside, valve-motion inside: North-Eastern V class 4–4–2 (*Author's collection*)

Cylinders and valve-motion outside: French Liberation or 141R class 2–8–2 (*Brian Hollingsworth*)

Lastly, there are lesser mechanisms which just need a drop or two of oil from an oil can—of normal shape, but three times normal size— just as one would put a little on door-hinges at home.

For a regular driver, this complex business of lubrication and examination is further complicated by differences between one class of locomotive and another; the methods described above apply quite differently to different classes. Of course the number and arrangement of wheels varies, but also the motion can be totally outside the wheels or totally inside. Or the cylinders and driving rods can be outside and the valve mechanism inside—or even vice-versa; or cylinders *and* valve gear both inside *and* outside. Some locomotives of the same class may have roller-bearings, for instance, and others not, requiring quite different lubrication treatment. Fortunately, in

Blue Peter takes water: note the driver working the valve on the ground, while the fireman is on the tender observing the water contents gauge (*Maurice Burns*)

Facing page:
American style water columns can be turned off from the top of the tender (*Jim Shaughnessy*)

our dream we have only one locomotive to deal with and that of the easiest type with two cylinders and motion outside.

Filling up

One chore has been spared us, for the oil tank is full and therefore we shall not have to tackle the business of refuelling with several thousand gallons of oil; a process which sounds easy but, in fact, is tricky for anyone who has not done it often enough to have gained the knack. On the other hand the tender tank does need filling with even more thousands of gallons of water, a process which needs nice co-operation between driver and fireman but is a little less fraught for novices than refuelling, if only because it is a lot less unpleasant to get soaked with water than oil.

The water column on this track is a little further up, so we move *Forward* and spot her so that the tender filler hole at the back of the tender comes opposite the water supply; next, mid-gear hand-brake on, cocks open and both of us down on the ground. The fireman's job is to climb the ladder to the top of the tender, open the suprisingly heavy lid and, having pulled the leather feed hose across with the chain provided, insert it into the tender. The driver works the king-size water valve down below on the ground and allows the tank to fill. Hopefully he will receive a cry or signal from the man on top in time to turn off the supply before Niagara begins.

4

GRAND JUNCTION EXPRESS

OUT ON THE LINE

The rule book

Now it is time to take our iron steed out of the locomotive yard and back her on to the train. At once we have a further unfamiliar thing to cope with; this time it is the rule book. Even before this we have been under its firm direction, although employees of modern railways no longer have to obey rules like the following . . .

'Railway servants not on duty on Sundays are expected to attend divine service. This will be the means of promotion should vacancies occur.'

On the other hand such rules as 'employees MUST NOT consume intoxicating liquor while on duty' apply with equal force to locomotive drivers today.

Movements in non-signalled areas such as locomotive yards are also covered by rules but they could be summed up in the expression *sauve qui peut*. The working of trains is a very different matter and even before we got on to the engine there were rules which should have been obeyed, such as for us to attend on time and examine notices posted telling of such things as special restrictions of speed on the lines over which the train is to be worked. And once on the engine and in charge, it is not to be left.

Before moving the engine, tools and (if we had been a coal-burner) fire-irons are placed so that they will not fall off. Various items must be on the engine: oil-lamps (for emergencies if electrics fail), detonators, a bucket (!) and tools. The prescribed identification lights, discs or indicators must be exhibited and, if neccessary, lit. If the driver is not thoroughly acquainted with the line he is going to run over, he must ask for a competent conductor. We in our dream are fortunate in finding we do know the road.

The first move we have to make is backwards out of the yard across on to the down main line. There is about a mile to go before arriving at the terminus where our train awaits us. The term 'down' needs some explanation. This railway has British-style rules, permanent way and signalling and in Britain direction is indicated by the terms 'down' and 'up'; the down direction is usually that leading away from the principal place on the line. Hence you go up to Scotland in a 'down' train. No doubt the term arose on early pre-1830 coal-hauling,

Facing page:
An oil lamp placed above the electric head light indicates the code for 'engine running light' (*Rodney Wildsmith*)

pit-to-port lines, where trains which started from the principal source of traffic literally ran down-hill.

Our particular iron horse, the design of which is of purely American inspiration, would be more at home on a West-bound or East-bound main; whilst one of those elegant and complex French *machines à vapeur* would have been happier with *pair* or *impair* (even or odd), referring not to *roulette* but to the numbers used for trains in the timetable, which are odd or even according to direction.

Headlight code

The first thing to do before moving is to set up the lights and, accordingly, following three other rules; the first specifies that an engine running light must carry a tail lamp. The other two concern engines fitted with electric lights; we must switch on the prescribed front light code for an engine running on its own (one lamp above the centre of the front buffer beam). If it had been daylight a white disc or unlit lamp would have been placed in that position and if our locomotive had not been fitted with electric light we would have used an oil lamp. The second rule specifies that an oil tail-lamp must be placed at the rear. This lamp will have a red shade in place—at one time apprentice firemen used to get sent to the stores to draw red oil for the tail-lamps. Of course, for this backing movement, the terms front and rear refer to the back of the tender and the front of the locomotive respectively.

Rule book detail

Incidentally, the 1950 British rule book, covering steam days, had 239 rules covering everything from 'Stationery, waste of' (Rule 3) to 'Insane persons' (Rule 166). The rules governing drivers are amongst the most complex. The notorious Rule 55 which concerns trains standing at signals has twelve clauses further divided into sub-sections. And that simple rule about bringing detonators on to the engine leads to a further five rules (twelve clauses) about handling them. What to do with them is yet another group. In any case all this is only the tip of the iceberg; when, for example, the rules speak of the prescribed light codes, reference is being made to both the general and to the various local appendices to the rule book, great bible-like books in their own right, full of 'musts' and 'must nots'.

Signals

It's a relief to return to something nice and easy, like setting our engine in motion, but almost immediately we encounter the fixed signal which governs the exit from the yard. Signal engineers are sometimes unkindly (and unjustly) referred to as mere lights-on-sticks men but, in fact, this light-on-a-stick thing called a colour-light signal is backed by some very sophisticated electrics so that drivers can have complete confidence that when it shows a colour other than red it is safe to proceed. It shows a very bright and uncompromising red just now and the rule book says that the fireman should descend from the engine and call the signal box from the telephone provided and tell the signalman who he is. 'Engine 1555 for the 8·30 at signal D328B,' you say and almost immediately the signal changes to yellow then green.

Out into the big world

Open the regulator with a touch on the oil latch to match and we roll out into the big world. The fact of the signal changing to green has not only proved electrically that all points are correctly set but also that the line is clear and even that the next signal we meet will not be at danger. If the signal had shown yellow, it would have been a caution that the next signal could show stop, ie, red. The rules say that we should observe all signals, keep a good look-out and sound the whistle to warn anyone in the way; just normal common-sense for a driver of any vehicle from a dog-cart to a super-tanker.

The next signal shows yellow and I as the driver close the regulator, you as the fireman matching this with reducing movement of the oil control and a small opening of the blower. Otherwise another rule concerning the emission of smoke from engines would have broken; not too visible in the dark, but if it happened in such a public place as the approach to this terminus during daylight, we might have to anwer for it on the superintendent's carpet.

The lights of Penzance station under its overall roof are now visible just ahead as we come to a stand under a red light on a signal bridge spanning all the tracks. Just beyond is the complex point-work of the station throat. Then 'P1' comes up in the lights and below the red light we see two diagonally placed white ones. This is a 'calling-on' indication showing that we can proceed to platform No. 1, but dead slow and only so far as the line is clear. This is exactly what we would expect as, of course, the train we are to haul will be standing at that platform ready for its locomotive.

Screw couplings, brake and steam heat pipes between locomotive and train (*British Rail*)

A coach end showing automatic couplers (*British Rail*)

11 Westinghouse automatic brake applied to engine tender and carriage

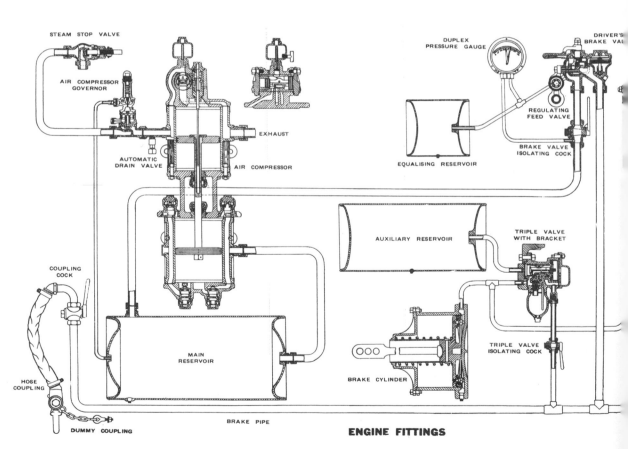

STEAM STOP VALVE

AIR COMPRESSOR GOVERNOR

AUTOMATIC DRAIN VALVE

EXHAUST

AIR COMPRESSOR

DUPLEX PRESSURE GAUGE

DRIVER'S BRAKE VALVE

REGULATING FEED VALVE

BRAKE VALVE ISOLATING COCK

EQUALISING RESERVOIR

AUXILIARY RESERVOIR

TRIPLE VALVE WITH BRACKET

COUPLING COCK

TRIPLE VALVE ISOLATING COCK

BRAKE CYLINDER

HOSE COUPLING

MAIN RESERVOIR

DUMMY COUPLING

BRAKE PIPE

ENGINE FITTINGS

Only 22 out of over 22,000
BR locomotives ever had
automatic couplers—the A4
class Streamline Pacifics
(*Author's collection*)

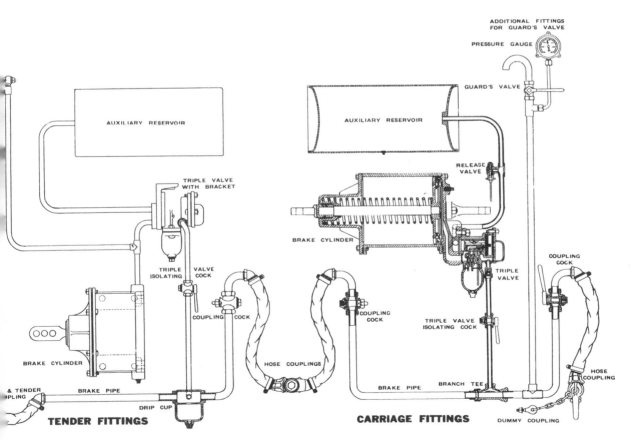

ADDITIONAL FITTINGS
FOR GUARD'S VALVE

PRESSURE GAUGE

GUARD'S VALVE

AUXILIARY RESERVOIR

AUXILIARY RESERVOIR

RELEASE
VALVE

TRIPLE VALVE
WITH BRACKET

BRAKE CYLINDER

COUPLING
COCK

TRIPLE
VALVE

TRIPLE
VALVE

VALVE
ISOLATING   COCK

COUPLING
COCK

COUPLING   COCK

COUPLING
COCK

TRIPLE VALVE
ISOLATING COCK

BRAKE CYLINDER

HOSE
COUPLING

HOSE COUPLINGS

& TENDER
PLING

BRAKE PIPE

DRIP CUP

BRAKE PIPE

BRANCH TEE

DUMMY COUPLING

TENDER FITTINGS

CARRIAGE FITTINGS

Correct attire is desirable. Japanese drivers' uniform supplied to the author for riding steam locomotives there. Note the British-style semaphore signal in background (*Brian Hollingsworth*)

The big engine goes clanking, grinding and shrieking over the sharp curves, points and crossings leading to the platform 1 line. I give her little blips of steam, enough just to keep her rolling but keeping in mind that too little and she might stall on the curves where friction is considerable. One hand strays from the brake handle. Very nice judgement is needed for the next bit; we want to stop just as we touch the train—with a sufficient 'clonk' to engage the automatic couplers, but insufficient to jar people in the cars. The fireman now has to get down and go back to the rear of the tender, connect up the air hose and the steam hose (surprisingly difficult the first few times), open the interconnecting cocks on both locomotive and train, then go round to the front of the locomotive to remove the tail lamp.

Coupling up

You must thank whoever dreamed up this dream that on this British railway the trains are American. Only twenty-two out of over 22,000 standard-gauge locomotives that British Rail have owned had or have automatic couplers—the famous streamliners on the East Coast route, the A4 class, 'streaks' as they were often called. To couple up any of the rest, a fireman (or second-man as he would now be called) would have to get down between the platform and the buffers and in a confined space couple up with an awkward, heavy and usually filthy screw coupling.

Air brakes

The next thing is to activate the brakes down the train. By force of law, since a few years before the turn of the century and in both Britain and North America, passenger trains (in the USA all trains) have had to have a brake which would meet three requirements:

1. Must be capable of application to every vehicle on the train
2. Must be capable of being applied both on the locomotive and from the train
3. Must be self-applying if the train becomes involuntarily divided.

Air pressure in a pipe running down the train was the only practicable means of braking either in the form of positive pressure (air brakes) or negative (vacuum brakes). The brakes on this train, (see Fig 11) are of the former type and operate on a system invented and developed by an American called George Westinghouse and often called after him. In order to make the brake self-applying if the train divides, air is not supplied direct from the train-pipe to the brake cylinders. Instead, it goes via a reservoir on each vehicle. A very clever device called a triple valve applies air from the reservoirs to the brakes if the air pressure in the train pipe becomes reduced, either when someone (normally the driver) does so deliberately or if a part of the train breaks away. To release the brakes the driver raises the air pressure in the train pipe, the triple valves then letting air out of the brake cylinders. At the same time the reservoirs on the train are then connected up, again through the triple valve, and re-charged by air from the train pipe.

Because the train will be standing in the station with brakes on, the first thing we will have to do is to release the brakes, by pushing the operating lever to the release position. Air goes from the main reservoir into the train pipe, pressure dropping in the former and rising in the latter. The drop in pressure of the main reservoir causes the governor valve of the steam-operated air pump to open and the air pump itself to begin working with a satisfying sis-phutt, siss-phutt, siss-phutt .... The platform line being level, the brakes can be released completely well before the start, the tender handbrake being applied.

The working timetable

Ah yes ... here is the guard of the train, reporting that it consists of sixteen vehicles weighing 820 tons and also that the brakes are working right to the rear of the train—he has an application valve in his van. We are attired correctly in enginemen's overalls and he makes no comment except to tell us there is an extra stop at Cambourne tonight—term's end at that Eton of the tunnelling world, the Camborne School of Mines. The stop is provided for conditionally in the working book, of course; the public timetable just says 'calls on request to pick up sleeping car passengers only'. Working book, what's that ... surely not another one? Yes, indeed, not one but three big tomes stuffed with essential information. The working book is more formally the Employees' Service Timetable and each railway Division has its own volume—our 200 mile journey covers three.

You might glance at four essential pages of the Plymouth Division timetable that now guides us, Fig 12. First there is a table of mileages and the gradients to be encountered against a list of places on the line, stations, sidings, level crossings and lone signal boxes. Our schedule comes next with separate columns for arrival and departure at each place. At places where we are not booked to stop, the passing time straddles the arrival and departure columns. Next there is a list of places where speed must be reduced for curves and for other engineering reasons. Some are shown as having indicator boards provided, others you just have to know ... then there is a list of the opening hours of signal boxes—many can be and are switched out, particularly at night.

Another page is entitled 'Engine Restrictions', that is, it lists lines on which different types of locomotives are or are not permitted to work. Dreams have their absurdities, because *Forward's* height (but not its weight) would make the type totally and universally prohibited, even on such a line as the Cornwall Railway, which once upon a time was laid to I.K. Brunel's famous Broad Gauge and hence had more room than normal under bridges and in tunnels. (Brunel's railways permitted 15 ft 6 in. height and 11 ft width, but since the passing of the broad gauge in 1892 they have been widely encroached upon.)

Strangely enough, this dream use of locomotives of American

Up Trains. PENZANCE AND TOTNES. Week Days.

Distance from Penzance M. C.	STATIONS	Ruling Gradient 1 in	Allow for Stop.	Allow for Start. §	"C"	"D"	"E"	"F"	"H", "J", "K"	Klingsford Junction Freight via Yate Junction. MO arr.	dep.	Empty C'ches. MX dep.	MO dep.	Empty C'ches. C dep.

Stations listed:
PENZANCE (Passenger), Ponsandane, Penzance (Goods), Long Rock, Marazion, St. Erth, Hayle, Gwinear Road, Camborne, Roskear Junction, Dolcoath Siding, Carn Brea, Carn Brea Yard, Redruth Junction, Redruth, Drump Lane, Scorrier, Wheal Busy Siding, Chacewater, Baldhu, Penwithers Junction, Probus, Probus & Ladock Ptfm., TRURO, Grampound Road, Burngullow, Trenance Siding, Trenance Junction, St. Austell, Par Harbour, Par, Treverrin, Lostwithiel, Bodmin Road, Largin, Doublebois, Liskeard, Menheniot, Trerule, St. Germans, Wearde, Saltash, Royal Albert Bridge, St. Budeaux West, St. Budeaux (Ferry Rd.), St. Budeaux East, Keyham, Ford Halt, Dockyard Halt, Devonport (Albert Rd.), Devonport Junction, Cornwall Junction, PLYMOUTH, NORTH ROAD, Mannamead, Lipson Junction, Laira Junction, Tavistock Junction, Plympton, Hemerdon, Cornwood, Ivybridge, Bittaford Platform, Wrangaton, Brent, Rattery, Stop Board 226m. 9jc., Tigley, Totnes, Ashburton Junction, NEWTON ABBOT.

Special Freight, Ordinary Freight and Vacuum-fitted Ballast Trains, when running out of course, will run at the standard point-to-point times shown herein (see also page 157) unless otherwise ordered. The time allowances shown for stopping and starting are to apply at places where calling for traffic purposes, but not to delay the train. §—Two minutes allowed for "C," "D" and "E" Head Code trains.

Up Trains.

STATIONS	Engine. G SO dep.	Paddington Passenger. A SO	Paddington Passenger. A	10.15 a.m. Newquay to Paddington Passenger. A SO	Empty Auto. B SO	Passenger. B	Trans. fer. K SO	Passenger. B	9.40 a.m. Newton Abbot New. quay Motor. K	Trans. fer K

Stations listed (same sequence as above): PENZANCE (Pass.), Ponsandane, Penzance (Goods), Long Rock, Marazion, St. Erth, Hayle, Gwinear Road, Camborne, Roskear Junction, Dolcoath Siding, Carn Brea, Carn Brea Yard, Redruth Junction, Redruth, Drump Lane, Scorrier, Wheal Busy Siding, Chacewater, Baldhu, Penwithers Junction, TRURO, Probus, Probus & Ladock Ptfm., Grampound Road, Burngullow, Trenance Siding, Trenance Junction, St. Austell, Par Harbour, Par, Treverrin, Lostwithiel, Bodmin Road, Largin, Doublebois, Liskeard, Menheniot, Trerule, St. Germans, Wearde, Saltash, Royal Albert Bridge, St. Budeaux West, St. Budeaux (Ferry Rd.), St. Budeaux East, Keyham, Ford Halt, Dockyard Halt, Devonport (Albert Rd.), Devonport Junction, Cornwall Junction, PLYMOUTH, NORTH ROAD, Mannamead, Lipson Junction, Laira Junction, Tavistock Junction, Plympton, Hemerdon, Cornwood, Ivybridge, Bittaford Platform, Wrangaton, Brent, Rattery, Stop Board 226m. 9jc., Tigley, Totnes, Ashburton Junction, NEWTON ABBOT.

U—When this train requires assistance beyond Hemerdon, the assistant engine to go through to Newton Abbot West Box. Y—The assistant engine to work through to Newton Abbot East Up Home Signal (Through Road). §—Advertised to arrive North Road 12.10 p.m.

12 Extracts from the Plymouth Division working timetable

SPEED OF TRAINS THROUGH JUNCTIONS AND AT OTHER SPECIFIED PLACES.

Inspectors, Signalmen and others must report to their Superior Officer every case in which trains run in excess of the speed limits shewn below, and full particulars must be forwarded at once to the Divisional Superintendent or District Traffic Manager.

NOTE. The speed of all Light Engines or Trains entering or leaving all Bay, Engine, Carriage, Avoiding Lines and Goods Loop Junctions must be restricted to 10 miles per hour except where restricted to a lower speed in the following list or elsewhere.

Name of Place.	Direction of Train. From	Direction of Train. To	Miles per hour.
DOWN MAIN LINE.			
Ashburton Junction	Branch Line	Main Line	15
Totnes Station	All Down Trains through	Platform Line	15
West of Totnes, 223 m.p. to 227m. 30ch.	All Down Trains	..	60
East and West of Brent, 229m. 50c. to 230½ m.p.	All Down Trains	..	50
East and West of Bittaford, 232m. 70c. to 233m. 10c.	All Down Trains	..	50
East and West of Ivybridge, 234¾ m.p. to 235½ m.p.	All Down Trains	..	40§
East and West of Cornwood, 237m.10c. to 239m.10c.	All Down Trains	..	50
Plympton Station, 241¾ m.p. to 242 m.p.	All Down Trains	..	60
Tavistock Junction, 243 m.p. to 243m. 8c.	All Down Trains over Curve	in Down Main Line	45
Tavistock Junction, 243m. 8c. to 243m. 18c.	All Down Trains	..	35 §
Tavistock Junction	Branch Line	Main Line	10
Laira Junction, 243m. 78c. and 244m. 4c.	All Down Trains	..	40 §
Lipson Junction	No. 1 Curve	Main Line	15
Mutley to Devonport, 245m. 50c. to 247½ m.p.	All Down Trains	..	25 §
North Road Station	All Down Trains through	Nos. 2 & 4 Platforms	20
North Road Station West Box to Millbay Box	All Down Trains	..	25
Approaching Millbay Station	Millbay Box	Millbay Station	5
Millbay Box to Millbay Docks (East Quay)	All Down Trains	..	10
Cornwall Junction 247½ m.p. to Cornwall Loop Junction 247¾ m.p.	Millbay	Devonport Junction	25 §
Devonport Junction	Main Line	Devonport S.R.	20
East and West of Devonport Station, 247m. 70c. to 248¾ m.p.	All Down Trains		30 §
Over Royal Albert Bridge, 250¾ m.p. to 251m. 23c.	All Down Trains	..	15
West end of Royal Albert Bridge to East end of Defiance Halt, 251m. 23c. to 252 m.p.	All Down Trains	..	35
East end of St. Germans Station to West end of St. Germans Station, 256½ m.p. to 256¾ m.p.	All Down Trains	..	40 §
Menheniot, 261m. 30c. to 261m. 50c.	All Down Trains	..	50
West of Liskeard Station, 265½ m.p. to 265m. 50c.	All Down Trains	..	50
Doublebois and Bodmin Road, 269 m.p. to 270m. 60c.	All Down Trains	..	45 §
Doublebois and Bodmin Road, 270m. 60c. to 274m. 20c.	All Down Trains	..	50 §
Lostwithiel Station, 277½ m.p. to 277¾ m.p.	All Down Trains	..	45
Lostwithiel, West end of Station	Main Line	Lostwithiel and Fowey Branch	10
East End of Par Stn., 281m. 40c. to 281m. 60c.	All Trains	..	45
East End of Par Station—Main Line to Branch Platform	All Trains	..	10
Burngullow and Grampound Road, 290 m.p. to 291 m.p.	All Down Trains	..	55
Grampound Road and Truro, 295 m.p. to 296 m.p.	All Down Trains	..	55
Truro Station	Roads between Platforms	..	30
Chacewater, 305m. 50c. to 306½ m.p.	All Down Trains	..	50 §
Chacewater Branch Platform	Truro	Chacewater	10
Redruth, 309m. 60c. to 310m. 10c.	All Down Trains	..	35 §
East and West of Gwinear Road, 315¾ m.p. to 316 m.p.	All Down Trains	..	40 §
East and West of Hayle, 319m. 30c. to 319m. 50c.	All Down Trains	..	45
St. Erth Junction	Main Line	St. Ives Branch	15
326m. 40c. to Penzance Station	All Down Trains	..	5
UP MAIN LINE.			
St. Erth Junction	St. Ives Branch	Main Line	15
West and East of Hayle, 319m. 50c. to 319m. 30c.	All Up Trains	..	45
West and East of Gwinear Road, 316 m.p. to 315¾ m.p.	All Up Trains	..	40 §
Redruth Station, 310m. 10c. to 309¾ m.p.	All Up Trains	..	35 §
Chacewater, 306½ m.p. to 305m. 50c.	All Up Trains	..	50 §
Truro Station	Between Platforms	..	30
Truro Station	Up Platform Line	..	15
East End of Par Stn., 281m. 60c. to 281m. 40c.	All Trains	..	45
East End of Par Station—Branch Platform to Main Line	All Trains	..	10
Lostwithiel, West end of Station	Lostwithiel and Fowey Branch	Main Line	10
Lostwithiel Station, 277¾ m.p. to 277½ m.p.	All Up Trains	..	45
West and East of Bodmin Road, 274½ m.p. to 272m. 10c.	All Up Trains	..	50
West of Doublebois, 270m. 50c. to 270m. 30c.	All Up Trains	..	45

THE SPEED OF UP AND DOWN TRAINS BETWEEN R.A. BRIDGE AND PENZANCE MUST NOT IN ANY CASE EXCEED 60 MILES PER HOUR.

§ Permanent Restriction of Speed Boards provided.

Speed of Trains through Junctions and at other Specified Places—continued.

NAME OF PLACE.	DIRECTION OF TRAIN. From	DIRECTION OF TRAIN. To	Miles per Hour.
UP MAIN LINE—continued.			
West of Doublebois, 269½ m.p. to 269 m.p.	All Up Trains	..	45
Doublebois and Liskeard, 265m. 50c. to 265½ m.p.	All Up Trains	..	50
East of Menheniot, 261m. 50c to 261m. 30c.	All Up Trains	..	50
West and East of St. Germans Station, 256¾ m.p. to 256½ m.p.	All Up Trains	..	40 §
East End of Defiance Halt to West End of Royal Albert Bridge, 252 m.p. to 251m. 23c.	All Up Trains	..	35 §
Over Royal Albert Bridge, 251m. 23c. to 250¾ m.p.	All Up Trains	..	15
West and East of Devonport Station, 248¾ m.p. and 247m. 70c.	All Up Trains	..	30 §
Devonport Junction	Devonport S.R.	Main Line	20
Cornwall Loop Jct., 247¾ m.p. to Cornwall Jct.	Devonport Junction	Millbay	25 §
Millbay Box to Cornwall Junction	All Up Trains	..	25
Leaving Millbay Station	Millbay Station	Millbay Box	5
Millbay Docks (East Quay) to Millbay Box	All Up Trains	..	10
Cornwall Jct. to North Road Station West Box	Millbay	North Road	25 §
Devonport to Mutley, 247½ m.p. to 245m. 50c.	All Up Trains	..	25 §
North Road Station	All Up Trains through Pla	tform Line (Nos. 6, 7, 8)	20
Lipson Junction	Main Line	No 1 Curve	15
Laira Junction, 244m. 4c. to 243m. 78c.	All Up Trains	..	40 §
Tavistock Junction, 243m. 18c. to 243m. 5c.	All Up Trains	..	35 §
Tavistock Junction	Main Line	Branch Line	10
Plymtpon Station	All Up Trains	..	60
Hemerdon and Cornwood, 239m. 10c. to 237m. 10c.	All Up Trains	..	50
West and East of Ivybridge, 235½ m.p. to 234¾ m.p.	All Up Trains	..	50
West and East of Bittaford, 233m. 10c. to 232m. 70c.	All Up Trains	..	50
West and East of Brent, 230½ m.p. to 229m. 50c.	All Up Trains	..	50
West of Totnes, 227m. 30 c. to 223 m.p.	All Up Trains	..	50
Totnes Station	All Up Trains through Plat	form Line.	15
Ashburton Junction	Main Line	Branch Line	15
BRANCH LINES.			
Ashburton Branch.			
The speed of trains over the Branch must not	exceed 40 miles per hour and	be further restricted as follows	:—
Ashburton Junction	Main Line	Branch Line	15
Ashburton Junction	Branch Line	Main Line	15
Buckfastleigh	Ashburton	Staverton	20
Kingsbridge Branch.			
The speed of trains over the Branch must not	exceed 35 miles per hour an	d be further restricted as follo	ws :—
Gara Bridge	Avonwick	Loddiswell	10
Gara Bridge	Loddiswell	Avonwick	15
Kingsbridge (between 12 m.p. and Kingsbridge)	All trains entering or leav	ing Station	15
Tavistock and Launceston Branch.			
The speed of all Up and Down trains between 45 miles per hour and for the remainder of	Lifton and Launceston, 27½ Branch 40 miles per hour, wi	m.p. and 31½ m.p., must not th the following further restrict	exceed ions :-
Tavistock Junction	Main Line	Branch Line	10
Tavistock Junction	Branch Line	Main Line	10
Bickleigh	All Up Trains	..	20
Yelverton	All Up Trains	..	20
Horrabridge	All Down Trains	..	20
Tavistock	All Up and Down Trains	..	20
Lydford	All Up Trains	..	20
Lydford and Coryton (between 19m. 40c. and 22 m.p.)	All Up and Down Trains	..	35
Princetown Branch.			
The speed of trains over the Branch must not	exceed 20 miles per hour	and be further restricted as foll	ows :—
Yelverton	Tavistock Branch	Princetown Branch	10
Yelverton	Princetown Branch	Tavistock Branch	10
Plymouth Curve No. 1.			
Lipson Junction	Main Line	No. 1 Curve	15
Lipson Junction	No. 1 Curve	Main Line	15
Mount Gould Junction	Lipson Junction	Friary Junction	20
Mount Gould Junction	Friary Junction	Lipson Junction	20
Mount Gould Junction	Lipson Junction	Cattewater Junction	20
Mount Gould Junction	Cattewater Junction	Lipson Junction	20
Friary Junction	Mount Gould Junction	Friary	20
Friary Junction	Friary	Mount Gould Junction	20
Yealmpton Branch.			
The speed of all trains over the Branch not to	exceed 30 miles per hour.		
Devonport Junction.	Main Line	Devonport (S.R.)	20
	Devonport (S.R.)	Main Line	20

§—Permanent Restriction of Spee' Boards provided.

ENGINE RESTRICTIONS.

The Standard Instructions relative to the working of engines in steam coupled together and assistance or double heading of trains, shewn in the General Appendix, subject to any local modifications shewn in this Service Time Table, must be observed.

MAIN LINE.

Totnes to Keyham (inclusive) .. .. All types authorised.
Keyham (exclusive) to Penzance .. All types authorised except 60XX (Kings) and 47XX.

Station.	Connections and Sidings.	Class of Engines prohibited.
Totnes	Quay Line	60XX, 47XX.
Totnes	Goods Shed and Weighbridge	42XX, 52XX, 47XX, 60XX, 72XX.
Brent	Connections to Spur. Down Siding West end .. Crossover Road, East end ..	42XX, 52XX, 47XX, 60XX, 72XX. Speed of 60XX engines not to exceed 5 m.p.h. when using this crossover.
Wrangaton	Sidings adjacent to Up Refuge Siding, Mileage Sidings and Shunt Spur on Up Side of Line.	60XX ("Kings")
Ivybridge	Up side loading bank and dead end	42XX. 47XX, 52XX, 60XX, 72XX.
Cornwood	Connection to Mileage Siding, West end	42XX, 47XX, 52XX, 60XX, 72XX.
Plympton	Clay Loading Bank and Cattle Pens ..	42XX, 47XX, 52XX, 30XX, 28XX. 72XX, Austerity 2–8–0 L.M.R. 2–8–0. (These engines can only put off or pick up traffic from either end of bank, 47XX West End only.)
Millbay	Crossover between Nos. 2 and 3 Platforms, Fish Loading Bank and Carriage Shute Siding.	60XX, 94XX. 28XX, 30XX, 42XX, 47XX, 52XX, 60XX, 72XX, Austerity 2–8–0, L.M.R. 2–8–0.
Millbay Goods ..	Scissors Crossover at entrance to Shed ..	52XX, 47XX, 72XX, 60XX.
Millbay Docks ..	All Lines and Sidings	60XX.
	Connections to back of Glasgow Wharf ..	All 4–6–0 type engines.
Devonport	Siding behind Signal Box	60XX "Kings," also 28XX, 30XX, 42XX, 47XX, 52XX, 72XX, Austerity 2–8–0, L.M.R. 2–8–0, 94XX.
	Crossover West End	All 4–6–0 types, also 28XX, 30XX, 42XX, 47XX, 52XX, 72XX, Austerity 2–8–0, L.M.R. 2–8–0, 94XX.
Devonport Goods Yard ..	Siding adjoining Loading Bank and Dead End Siding nearest Tunnel.	All types except 33XX, 34XX and 90XX 4–4–0, and 45XX and 55XX—2–6–2T.
	Sidings Nos. 1 and 7, and connections to Cattle Pens and Goods Shed.	All 4–6–0 type, also 28XX, 30XX, 42XX, 47XX, 52XX, 60XX, 72XX, Austerity 2–8–0, L.M.R. 2–8–0, 94XX.
	Goods Shed	All 4–6–0 types and large engines with outside cylinders, 84XX, 94XX.
Keyham	Cattle Pens Road	47XX, 60XX, 84XX, 94XX.
	Admiralty Siding	Not more than two 60XX engines may back into this siding to stand just clear of locking-bar of points leading to dead end but not to use dead end siding.
	All W.R. Engines except those shewn in next column may work over Dockyard lines Barrack Gates to Exchange Sidings, through Outer road of Exchange Sidings and beyond for distance sufficient only for backing into siding adjoining the Outer road. Speed not to exceed 10 miles per hour.	47XX, 60XX.
St. Germans	Cattle Pens	All 4–6–0 type Engines, also 28XX, 43XX—73XX, Austerity 2–8–0, L.M.R. 2–8–0.
Liskeard	All classes may stand on Looe Branch Line up to 65 feet from clearance point of short dead end siding on Up side. Stop board provided.	
Burngullow	Parkyn & Peter's Siding	30XX, 36XX, 37XX. 42XX, 52XX, 57XX–97XX, 72XX, 84XX, 94XX, L.M.R. 2–8–0.
Grampound Road ..	Cattle Pens, Up side	4–6–0 types. All other types may work as far as Stop Board.
Truro	Carriage Shute, and Down Sidings East End.	4–6–0 types.
Redruth	Old Yard	28XX, 30XX, 42XX, 52XX, 72XX, Austerity 2–8–0, L.M.R. 2–8–0.
Redruth (Drump Lane) ..	Connection from Shunt Spur to Cattle Pens Road	All 4–6–0 type engines, also 28XX.
Hayle	Sidings adjacent to Refuge Siding ..	"Castle," 10XX, 40XX, 49XX, 59XX, 69XX, 68XX, 78XX, 29XX.
St. Erth	See St. Ives Branch	

BRANCHES.

Section of Line.	Engines Authorised.	Prohibitions.
Totnes to Ashburton ..	0–6–0T Uncoloured	—
	2–4–0T "Yellow"	—
	0–4–2T 48XX	—
	58XX	—
	2–6–2T 44XX	—
Brent to Kingsbridge ..	Uncoloured	20XX–21XX
	"Yellows"	
Tavistock Jct. to Yelverton, inclusive.	All classes except 60XX and 47XX.	Marsh Mills—Clay Works Siding.—No engine heavier than 45XX permitted.

The 4–6–0s whose typically American design was disguised by Victorian brass and copper work (*Colourviews Limited*)

During the build-up of men and equipment prior to 'D-day' in 1944, American-built 2–8–0s were found at work over parts of the Great Western Railway system; in September 1943 this USA locomotive was heading a freight train at Reading West Junction (*M. W. Earley*)

lineage on the Great Western line is a mere repetition of history. Around the turn of the century, British locomotive design took a great leap forward with the introduction by Locomotive Superintendent G. J. Churchward of a series of 4–6–0s whose typically American design was disguised by a lot of Victorian brass and copper work and distinguished by a very high standard of workmanship and finish. The *Saints*, as they were called, transformed train running on the Great Western Railway; their 462 almost identical successors, the *Halls*, *Granges* and *Counties*, stayed until dieselisation in the 1960s. As has been mentioned, numbers of them ran as oil-burners for a time shortly after World War II. During that conflict, too, large numbers of American-built 2–8–0s descended on the Great Western Railway.

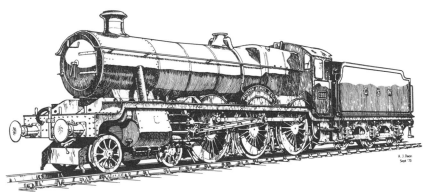

No. 6998 *Burton Agnes Hall*—GWR modified Hall class 4–6–0, preserved at Didcot, Berks

49

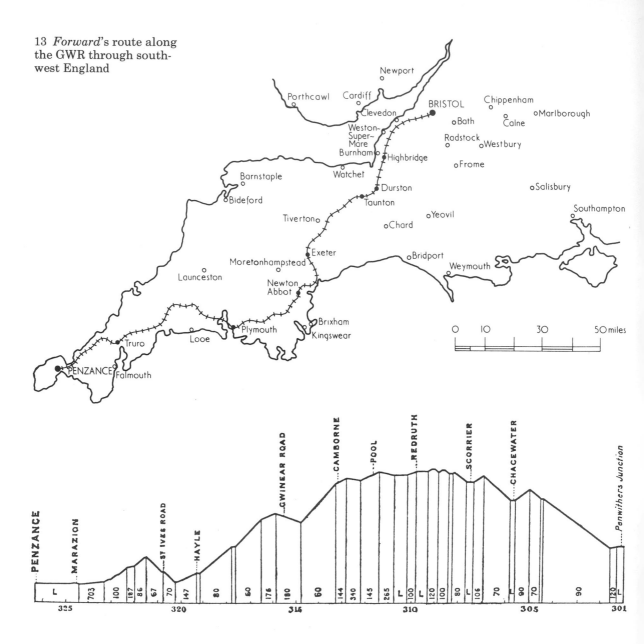

13 *Forward*'s route along the GWR through south-west England

14 Gradient profile from Penzance—St Ives Road is now called St. Erth (*Author's collection*)

The Weekly Notice

To a driver accustomed to working trains day in and day out on the line, the contents of the service timetable would be indelibly imprinted in his consciousness; but even he would have to look very hard at yet a further document, called the Weekly Notice. It is of innocuous magazine size, but as with scorpions, whose stinging power is in inverse proportion to their size, there is plenty of trouble in store for any engineman who has not read it with care. It tells of such things as temporary restrictions of speed for engineering work (in steam days very inadequately indicated on the ground, especially at night); major and minor permanent alterations to the railway;

Blue Peter displays the headlamp code for 'express passenger train' (*D. Cullen*)

places where clearances are temporarily obstructed by, for example, scaffolding at a bridge under repair and at which enginemen would be very unwise to look out. Whether it is something small, like a water column out of action or something big, such as diversions from the normal route or wrong-line working for repairs to the line (unlikely except on Sundays), it is all set out in the pages of the Weekly Notice. We note a 15 mph temporary speed restriction at Tavistock Junction—the worst possible place on the whole line, immediately before the dreaded Hemerdon incline.

Preparations to start

Traditionally, engine crews have little interest in what is hung on behind their locomotive's rear coupler, but in fact the Grand Junction Express is a luxury night train with through sleeping cars and carriages for most significant destinations north of Birmingham to the north. Our concern with it is to switch on the head-light code for 'express passenger train or breakdown train going to clear the line', one light at either end of the buffer beam, and to note the schedule of the train which the service timetable laconically calls the 8.30 pm Birmingham Passenger and see that the correct pressure (80 lb per sq. in) is maintained in the steam heating pipe. We shall be working as far as Bristol, see Fig 13, whence the train will be taken over by the London, Midland and Scottish Company, a concern whose foreign ways any true Great Western Railway man views with great suspicion—and *vice versa,* of course.

As departure time approaches, the task of working this great train successfully over 200 miles of highly difficult railway seems daunting in its complexity; we should do the same as we did earlier and take it in syllables. Our initial run is (see Fig 14) the 5 miles to St. Erth, junction for St. Ives; assuming that the signals are showing clear, the engine will have to be worked to accelerate the train on along the level beside Mount's Bay. The same applies to the short 1½ mile rise at between 1 in 80 and 1 in 90 which follows. We are in fact crossing Cornwall at its narrowest point, from tide-water to tide-water. This means a short sharp descent at 1 in 67 and nice judgement to make a

51

precise stop at St. Erth's platform. As we go over the summit, it is important to remember that the surface of the water in the boiler stays level with the earth rather than the locomotive. Accordingly, as the boiler tilts forward, the level goes down, quite drastically on this change from 1 in 85 up to 1 in 67 down. It is necessary to have the water right up to the top nut of the gauge going uphill, so that it can still be seen above the bottom nut going down. The nine minutes allowed from Penzance to St. Erth is very tight, but the minute or so we shall drop can be made up later, although the prim note in the timetable 'On this section of line time must not be made up by fast running down the inclines' has reason in it, as we shall find.

Right away!

It is now 8.29 and it is my duty—with an air of extreme nonchalance—to keep an eye out back along the train for the guard's right-away, signalled with a green hand-lamp from a point opposite his van at the rear. I have wound the reverser into full forward gear or 75% cut-off ready for the start. Whistles are blown and there's the green light . . . right-away mate. First a check that the starting signal is showing green, then release the engine-air brake and give a warning whistle. The regulator is eased open by pulling it backwards on its quadrant and after a moment's hesitation the wheels start to turn. It's a dry night, so slipping will be no problem, unless one is absurdly heavy handed with the throttle. After a few revolutions the cylinder cocks are closed and the regulator can be opened wide. You follow this movement with the oil latch and as speed rises I ease the reverser back to 45 then 25%. The colour-light signals show green all the way past Ponsandane carriage sidings and Long Rock Locomotive depot, where we were introduced to *Forward*. On the other side Mount's Bay and St. Michael's Mount glisten in the moonlight as we run along the shore. By Marazion speed has risen to 55 mph and the line swings round away from the sea. Now we leave the lights behind and begin to climb up into the darkness that shrouds the magic land of Cornwall. It suddenly seems no surprise that the last native wolf in England was killed in this very parish of Lugvan.

Cut-off

This cut-off business needs some further explanation. It is one in which the driver can exercise some considerable discretion. Further, there is no clear analogy with any of the controls on a motor car; if one did make one it would be some combination of changing gear and advancing or retarding the ignition.

There is no argument that one starts the locomotive in full gear, cutting off steam at 75% along each stroke of the pistons. This is because, if the cut-off point in full gear was any earlier the locomotive could easily be standing with the cranks in a position where no steam could reach the cylinders.

There is also no argument but that the cut-off should be made earlier in the stroke when moving at more than walking pace. The action of doing this is often referred to as 'linking-up' or 'notching up'. The latter is a reference to the days when the reversing gear on most locomotives was a big lever or pole, whose position was held by a latch working in notches on a quadrant.

A good analogy here is a door, which you must imagine that two people are trying to swing backward and forwards. If the door is heavy, to get it moving they need to push for nearly the whole of the swing; but once going it is much better for each pusher to give a short quick shove in the early part of the swing.

But by how much should the cut off be reduced? The text book says that the locomotive should normally be driven on full regulator and the cut-off reduced or increased by turning the reversing wheel in order to reduce or increase the power developed in the cylinders. The power which is developed would in its turn be limited either by the steam-raising capacity of the boiler or the speed required, ie, the amount needed. The actual amount of cut-off that the steam supply will cope with depends mainly on the speed. In simple terms, if you do not fill the cylinders so full you can fill them more often.

On the other hand, the same result can be achieved (at slightly greater cost) by setting a longer cut-off with the regulator opened or closed according to the demand for power—driving on the regulator as against driving on the reversing wheel. Some drivers prefer this method because the regulator is easier to adjust than some reversing gears; but we have reliable power-assisted cut-off adjustment with the Hadfield steam reverser.

The nominal amount of cut-off which has been set is indicated by that pointer on a scale which runs from 75% forward down to 0 (usually referred to as mid-gear and fairly analogous to neutral in a motor car) then on up to 75% back gear.

Gathering speed

As an American style locomotive, *Forward* has a powerful headlight; but, running on a British railway, headlights are not used. It seems at first sight utterly unsafe to run without seeing where you are going. This is before thinking a little deeper; then one realises that, on a train with a stopping distance of three-quarters of a mile or more, by the time you have seen an obstruction it is too late to stop. Furthermore, rail safety in steam days depended (and in some places still depends) on picking out oil lamps shining through the coloured spectacles of semaphore signals. Dazzled by the headlight of a train on the opposite line, drivers could easily miss a vital signal.

The summit (at milepost $319\frac{1}{4}$, though we can't see it) is breasted at 46 mph; shortly afterwards I shut the regulator and you respond with oil control and blower. Speed then rises rapidly on the 1 in 67 descent. The engine rides smoothly, but, now the moon is obscured, nothing prepares a stranger to the footplate for this blind and headlong descent into inky blackness.

5

SIGNALS IN THE NIGHT

A CHAPTER OF INCIDENTS

Light from an oil lamp shines through the glass (*Brian Hollingsworth*)

Automatic warning system—a ramp in the centre of the track is used to provide an audible signal in the cab (*British Rail*)

Semaphore signals

The first signal in the night is now approaching—the St. Erth Up Distant signal. Distant signals are 'caution' or 'warning' signals, in contrast to other signals which are 'stop' signals. For this reason you might think that a distant is less important than a stop signal. However, the contrary is true—a distant showing caution, being 'on' as the saying is, is the sign for the driver to take urgent steps to bring the speed of a fast running train down to walking pace, ready to stop immediately. It can take three-quarters of a mile or more to bring a fast train to a stand.

A semaphore signal is 'on' when the arm is horizontal—a symbolic barring of the way. It is 'off' or all-clear when the arm is inclined, whether upwards or downwards. Great Western signals go downwards, usually to a particularly steep angle. For night viewing there are two coloured glass spectacles as part of the arm. They are so arranged that the light from an oil lamp shines through the glass of the colour corresponding to the position of the arm. Green means all clear, although the spectacle is bluish to compensate for the yellowness of the oil light. Yellow glass is used for the other spectacle of a distant and red for that of a stop signal.

By day (or if the moon was out) a distant can be distinguished by a yellow instead of a red arm and a V-notch cut in the end. The stripe on the arm is black instead of white and matches the notch in shape.

People often dismiss semaphore signalling as crude—mere weighted arms connected to the signal box by wires. This is quite wrong; first the signalman cannot pull the lever to lower a distant signal until every relevant point and signal right through his station on the line in question is set and, if appropriate, locked; further, all opposing signals must be proved at danger. Second, once he has pulled off, nothing can be unlocked. There are also two independent electrical indicators in the signal box which show him firstly that the distant signal arm is actually in the position corresponding to his lever and secondly that the oil flame of the lamp is actually burning. On top of all this, there is the cab signalling system, known as AWS or Automatic Warning System, but originally (the Great Western had it system-wide a generation before anyone else) ATC or Automatic Train Control. In gratitude for its assistance drivers know it as 'our little friend in the corner'.

In semaphore territory, AWS only applies to distant signals and, by means of what were originally ramps in the centre of the track (nowadays it is done by magnets), gives an audible indication in the cab of the relevant signals aspect. A bell rings for clear; for caution, a siren sounds, the brakes being automatically applied at the same time.

All this leads to the fact that what we are looking for—and it is your duty to assist me—is a yellow or green light coming at us out of the darkness, while at the same time 'our little friend in the corner' gives a confirming indication. Between here and Bristol we shall pass 147 signal boxes and at the approach to each of these is the signal whose message is of such crucial importance to us. The train has to stop at St. Erth anyway, so the message of its distant signal is slightly academic; should it show caution we should merely have to be prepared to stop at the stop signal—called the 'home'—a few yards short of the platform.

Stopping
It is fair to say that at least as much—and possibly more— skill is needed to stop a train with the required precision and smoothness than to start and run it. The first thing is that the brake control works in an entirely different way to that on a motor car, even those which have power brakes. On a motor car you press the pedal and keep it pressed with the force required. On a train you move the handle only to increase or decrease the brake force.

The second thing is that, with 700 tons of locomotive and train streaming down hill, nice judgement is needed so that we avoid

The cab of a GWR oil-burning locomotive—'our little friend in the corner' is on the right-hand side (*British Rail*)

The signalman cannot pull
off any signal until all
points and conflicting
signals are correctly set
(*J. Ransom*)

overrunning the platform with all the embarassment and delay which
that entails or, just as bad, over-doing the braking force. In this latter
case the time is now just right to deposit soup in an important (and
vociferous) diner's lap. Or make wheels pick up and slide, causing
flats to form. You would describe the amount of brake force applied
by the amount of reduction in the train pipe air pressure, as recorded
on the brake gauge. A drawing of a typical brake valve is shown as
Fig 15.

There are five positions of the brake handle (see Fig 16)—in
clockwise order they are charge and release, running, lap, application and emergency. The release position we have already used to
release the brakes on the main train when we coupled up. The
running position is the one we are in now and the action required is to
pull the handle from the position across the lap position to the
application position, feel the brakes take hold and when they are on
hard enough, put the handle back to lap position.

An 8 lb per sq. in. reduction of the pressure in the train pipe will be
sufficient. We could now pull them on a little harder by a momentary
return to the application position or ease them off by going back to
the running position. It might even be necessary to release the brakes
completely by returning to the release position for a dozen seconds or
so and then going back to the running position.

The emergency or 'big-hole' position lets air out of the train pipe

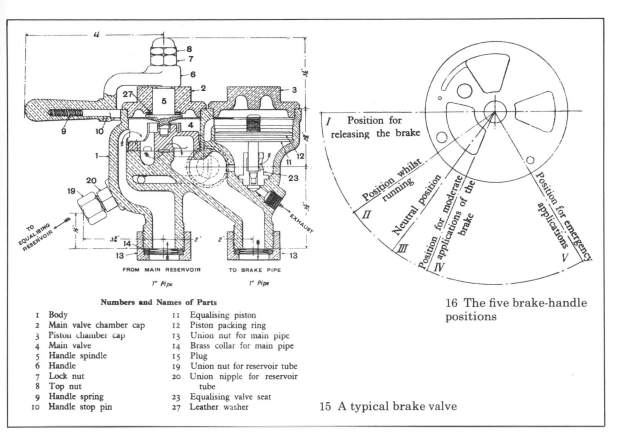

I Position for releasing the brake

Position whilst running

II

Neutral position

III

Position for moderate applications of the brake

IV

Position for emergency applications

V

16 The five brake-handle positions

FROM MAIN RESERVOIR   TO BRAKE PIPE

1" Pipe   1" Pipe

TO EQUALISING RESERVOIR

EXHAUST

Numbers and Names of Parts

1	Body	11	Equalising piston
2	Main valve chamber cap	12	Piston packing ring
3	Piston chamber cap	13	Union nut for main pipe
4	Main valve	14	Brass collar for main pipe
5	Handle spindle	15	Plug
6	Handle	19	Union nut for reservoir tube
7	Lock nut	20	Union nipple for reservoir tube
8	Top nut		
9	Handle spring	23	Equalising valve seat
10	Handle stop pin	27	Leather washer

15 A typical brake valve

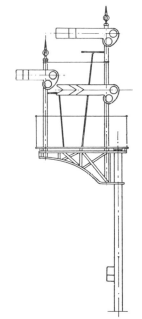

17 Diagram of a bracket signal—the left-hand arm controls access to a branch line (*Author's collection*)

rapidly through a large aperture. Big-holing is only used in circumstances where the braking must be as fierce as possible, regardless of minor damage to the train and its occupants. It is the furthest of the five positions round the spindle and this gives rise to the expression 'wiping the clock' when emergency braking is used in some desperate situation.

Our situation is by no means desperate; speed is falling steadily and the train is under good control when the St. Erth platform lights come into view. In fact, the brakes are eased off a little to make the precise stop at the end of the platform—the easing also helps to make the stop a smooth one. The deceleration has helped to give a false low water reading—but now it surges back, helped by the brief easing of the down gradient through the station. Whew . . .!

To get as much as possible of the long train alongside the platform we have run past the starting signal at the end. This is a double signal, (see Fig 17) with a subsidiary post and arm bracketed out from the main post. This lower arm controls entry to the St. Ives branch and does not concern us, but the main (higher) arm does and, of course, is pulled off, just as we were entitled to expect from seeing the distant at clear.

It is a nice easy start from St. Erth—downhill for half a mile, then a gruelling $4\frac{1}{2}$ mile climb, mostly at 1 in 61, to the next stop at Gwinear

Road. This will really clear the cobwebs out of the tubes. A 40 mph speed restriction—unmarked—though Hayle at the bottom of the dip is so near that it will not seriously incommode us. Meantime I wind the reverse into full gear.

A trespasser

With right-hand drive, as is normal GWR practice, you will have to watch for the guard's right-away. Or, since his van is way out of sight back round the curve, you look for it being relayed by platform staff. Right, there we go—brakes released, regulator open, oil latch up and off she marches. Acceleration is rapid with full regulator on the short down grade. Brake handle back to running position, cut-off set at 40% for the climb, injector on and we have nothing to do now except look out for distant signals at Hayle Wharf and Hayle—two boxes so close together that Hayle's distant is carried on the same post as Hayle Wharf's home. A succession of greens takes us through, across the viaduct and ... bloody hell ... there's a man walking with his back to us in the four-foot, that is, between the rails of the line we are on, caught in the lights of the street alongside.

I snatch at the whistle cord and the second or two before he steps aside—during which time we move more than 100 ft nearer him—seems like an age. Those unkind 'Trespassers will be Prosecuted' notices are not put up out of any toffee-nosed wish for privacy, but from a purely selfish desire on the part of the railway not to be involved in the messy deaths of foolish and thoughtless people.

Whilst the trespasser is, from the legal point of view, clearly in the wrong, a driver cannot help feeling responsible for any harm his engine may do; even though such feeling may be unjustified because in no way can a 700 ton train travelling at speed be stopped in a couple of hundred yards or so. The aftermath of a fatal accident of this kind is very serious—a driver who was involved would be put on the rack at three successive enquiries—the railway's, the Coroner's and the Ministry of Transport's; added to which there would be hours of delay for the train. Readers will understand the reason for the two words of 'Railroad Esperanto' which heralded this incident.

In fact, it at first quite spoilt our pleasure in the superb action of our fabulous locomotive all-out up grade with this tremendous train. So it is for six minutes—water level maintained and boiler pressure rock steady—when the siren note which is our little friend in the corner's way of saying 'look out' heralds the yellow-orange light of Gwinear Road West's distant at caution. There is a level crossing just beyond the platform and the signalman at the East Box prefers not to shut the gates until we are a good deal closer. This is a moment when a coal-fired engine would be almost bound to need to blow off a lot of steam through the safety valves. This is because on a coal-burner one can't just turn off the production of steam like a tap. A ton or so of white-hot fire takes a measurable time to die down. On the other hand, with oil the process is instantaneous; as I shut the regulator you bring back the oil latch and crack open the blower.

As we peer through the darkness for the light of the outer home

signal, an express runs by on the down main—the famous *Dutchman*, 1.30 pm from Paddington. The home is showing red but, as we approach, it drops, changing to green, appropriate for us to gently slow to a stop with the train at the platform and the locomotive straddling the level crossing beyond.

In respect of grades, the next little run to the conditional stop at Camborne is almost a carbon copy, on a slightly smaller scale, of that from St. Erth. Incidentally, while we stand waiting for the right-away, two bits of locomotive lore that have slipped in need some further explanation. The man at Hayle was described as walking in the 'four-foot'. This term is a shortening of '4 ft 8½ in. way' and refers to the space between two rails on which trains run; this is in contrast to the 'six foot' which means the space of this width between the inner rails of adjacent up and down lines. It gives about two feet clear between passing trains. On many Great Western routes which were once double-track 7 ft 0¼ in. gauge lines, the 'six-foots' are in fact 8 ft or more wide, but are still referred to by the same name.

Right- and left-hand drive
Right hand drive has been mentioned. The side on which the driver sits is governed by the positioning of some substantial ironmongery and a great deal of plumbing. In North America right-hand drive was nearly universal and corresponds to running on the right over double track. On the other hand our Chinese prototype has left-hand drive, corresponding to left-hand running in China. In Britain, and in spite of universal left-hand running, the old companies differed, some preferring one and some the other. When it came to new building, British Railways settled on the left-hand side for the driver, but there was little conversion of existing locomotives to the new standard.

Level crossings
Your view of the train for the guard's signal is excellent, because here the up platform is inside the curve, even though we are hanging out over the level crossing gates. It is a comfort to think that, where they cross on the level, railway and road traffic must be physically separated by these substantial barriers, interlocked with the signalling. A sad contrast to the situation at the thousands of farmer's level crossings, where the opening of the gates depends

The hazard of farmers' level crossings (*Author's collection*)

18 The emergency single-line at Carn Brea Junction

entirely on some non-railwayman's dubious hearing, sight and judgement ... but at least farmers won't be moving their animals after dark.

Camborne marks the beginning of the heavily industrialised Cornish tin-mining area, with seven signal boxes in four miles. For example, the distance from Camborne to Roskear Junction is a mere 15 chains (a chain, the unit used on the railway for fractions of a mile, is 22 yards, 1/80 of a mile, the length of a cricket pitch) although the latter, which gives access to a branch serving various works and mines, is normally switched out at this hour. This means that the signals of which it has exclusive control will be at clear and Camborne signal box will obtain the line clear from the next box—Dolcoath is its name—37 chains further on.

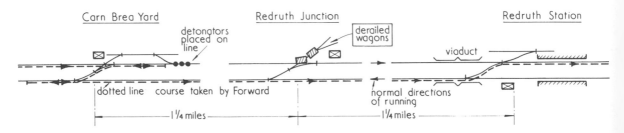

Obstruction—danger—emergency single line working

It is normal that most railway journeys, perhaps as many as ninety-nine out of a hundred, are quite without incident. This one is the hundredth, however, because as we stand in Camborne, the platform inspector comes up to warn us that there is something on the floor—he means a derailment—at Redruth Junction, blocking the up line and we will have to work on the wrong line past the obstruction from Carn Brea Junction to Redruth Station.

And so it proves to be; after a short level run, Carn Brea Station distant is found at danger and the home is lowered as we reach it, the signalman giving us a green hand-signal to indicate 'line clear but station or junction blocked' and we creep the mile or so on to Carn Brea Junction, to be brought to a stand at the home signal—Fig 18 opposite shows the situation.

The principle of this wrong line working is that a single appointed pilotman shall start or accompany all trains on the single line section. Since the pilotman cannot be at both ends at once, the possibility of head-on collision is avoided. Sure enough, a man climbs aboard, his identity clear from the red 'Pilotman' armband he wears round his sleeve.

Forward then draws forward with the train to clear the crossover road, you looking back for a red stop signal, given as the last coach clears the points. Ahead is a red lamp on the track and, although we can't see them, three detonators clipped to the rail. The explosion of these would be a last-ditch protection against the effects of any misunderstanding.

Passenger trains are not allowed to pass over any points in the facing direction, ie, the direction in which there is a choice of route, without these being locked or clamped. This can be provided for in the signalling, where facing movements are the normal thing, but here they are not normal and it is necessary to wait for the points to be clamped by hand. In the meantime, I wind the reverser into full back gear.

Right, there's the signal, a green hand-lamp waved to and fro horizontally; and very gently the train is set back on to the down line, over the violent reverse curve that forms the crossover. Once clear, again there is a wait for the points at the other end to be clamped, then away we go forwards on the down or right-hand line. The rule book says that trains must be run over the single line cautiously and at reduced speed and drivers must make frequent use of the whistle by giving a series of 'pop' whistles. All this we do.

At Redruth Junction we pass (at extreme caution) a couple of wagons sitting rather forlornly off the rails, awaiting the arrival of the breakdown crane. Shortly afterwards, at Redruth station, we are receiving a hand signal to cross over back to our own line. The pilotman drops off—he accompanied us because the next train to be passed over the single line section is one in the opposite direction, in fact the 3.30 pm ex-Paddington *Jubilee*—and once again the great engine strains at the couplings and we gather speed down the long descent towards Truro.

Permanent speed restriction

Soon we are running fast downhill with a mere breath of steam; not for long, however, as we look out for the illuminated '40' sign which marks the permanent restriction near Chacewater. There it is; so, the brakes go on and the long train swings easily round the curves— looking back we can see the winding river of light behind us.

Again speed rises and on this 1 in 82 down the force of gravity by itself is sufficient to maintain a speed higher than the line limit of 60 mph. Just a touch on the brake lever—letting barely a thimbleful of air out of the brake-pipe—suffices to check the excess speed. The regulator is held shut, blower and oil latch slightly open and the cut-off advanced a little to 25%.

Emergency speed restriction

The pleasureable excitement of this fast drifting descent ends— literally—with a bang as a detonator explodes under *Forward*'s leading wheels, accompanied by a yellow hand-held signal. This indicates an emergency speed restriction and, for us, the necessity for a full application of the brake. It subsequently transpires that the problem is a broken crossing rail at Penwithers Junction, where the Falmouth branch joins the main line; even up here in the cab the unusually severe clank over the junction points is noticeable. A green handsignal confirms that the trouble is now behind us, but with Truro tunnel and Truro station dead ahead, there is no scope to get up speed again. Shortly we come to rest in the platform.

An illuminated '40' sign marking a permanent 40 mph speed restriction (*P. M. Alexander*)

19 Gradient profile—Truro to Plymouth

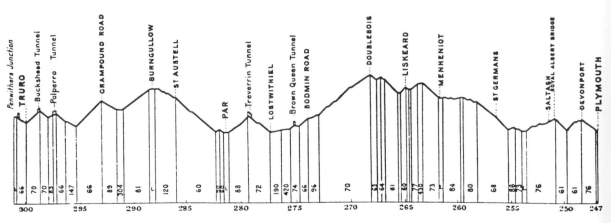

6

FASTER, FASTER

ONWARDS TO BRISTOL

They say troubles come in threes—so, hopefully, the three that have been thrown at us in thirty-five short miles will be our ration for the night. Our so-called grand express has so far stopped seven times, more often than any booked 'stopper' would—added to which we are almost thirty minutes down on schedule. Anyway, we now face what should be a fifty mile non-stop run to Plymouth. The river valleys of Cornwall run basically north and south so our progress will be a series of ups and downs, with thirteen separate summits, (see Fig 19). In most cases the valleys are crossed by magnificent viaducts, until we finally enter Devon over Brunel's famous Royal Albert bridge. There are ten major restrictions of speed, of which six are situated in dips or on down-grades, where they will affect us severely. Later on we shall tackle the seventy-five miles from Exeter to Bristol on which there is only one significant summit and only one significant speed restriction.

A flight plan

It is necessary to make what in the airline industry is called a flight plan. Of fuel we should have an ample amount for the whole journey, but water is a different matter. They take the dining car off the back of the train at Plymouth and while this is being done there will be time to refill the tender from the water column at the end of the platform. It is fortunate that the load is reduced because the worst inclines of the whole trip exist on the next section on to Newton Abbot. At this place the six-car Torbay section is added, making us up to twenty cars and 700 tons. There are water troughs at Exminster, from which we shall try and scoop a reasonable supply and similarly at a further thirty-eight miles further on, beyond Taunton; this should see us through to Bristol.

There is the question of winning a bit of time back and this is in some ways a bit of a poser. Over in France, engine crews receive a bonus for recovering lost time; a practice of which the risks were reduced by the use of a recording speedometer carried on the locomotive. Mindful, perhaps, of the fate of Casey Jones and his passengers, American and British managements never did anything as pointed as this to encourage drivers to make up time.

Nearly all steam locomotives have a capacity for being thrashed

and by doing this the run could be done in less than booked time. Fuel consumption and wear increase, but against that can be offset the fact that punctual running should bring in more in fares, although this night run is not too sensitive in this respect. If we had a coal-burner the faster running would involve us as well as the locomotive in harder work—a double dose. First, the extra speed involves more coal per mile; second, the faster speed involves less time per mile. Another factor which would not affect us, because we are not regulars, is a feeling that, should drivers demonstrate that they can do the run in less time than booked, soon enough the management will ask them to do it as a regular thing. Be all that as it may, we are going to have a go, aided (hopefully) by the signalmen along the line and the station staff at Plymouth and Newton Abbot.

Of the run to Plymouth sufficient to say that it is a series of carbon copies of the bits we have already done—but without the stops. There is no opportunity to make up more than a few odd seconds of time and, indeed, the regulator is closed and steam shut-off for nearly half the journey. Frequent corresponding movements with the oil latch and many applications of the brake for speed restrictions are our constant pre-occupation as before. We take advantage of the heavy blast on ascending gradients by throwing a scoop of sand into the firebox to scour clean the boiler tubes. This soot-removal process is needed every thirty miles or so.

Automatic warning system

A monotonous succession of green signal lights comes at us out of the darkness; in the case of distant signals, normally accompanied by the all-clear ring from the cab-signalling apparatus. The AWS system is designed 'fail-safe' and, accordingly, a few times the clear signal from the lineside is accompanied by the caution siren from the cab apparatus. Any fault or failure of contact gives the 'danger' indication. The book allows the lineside signal to govern our conduct and I accept its all-clear, pressing the 'cancel' handle provided on the side of the cab signalling box.

Viaducts and bridges

Crossing the many high viaducts is a great thrill especially from the left side where one looks down out of the cab to the moonlit base of the valley a hundred feet or more below. Finally, Brunel's great bridge—once described by a Victorian journalist as a 'double ferringuous bow'—comes into view as the train winds round the headland above the Hamoaze, where in steam days and before, a battle fleet could (and often did) lie at anchor. Such reflections must be set aside as the necessity comes for unfamiliar action. The bridge carries only a single line of rails—the only single line section on the journey—and the regulations state that on single lines the driver must, in addition to seeing clear signals, be given a physical token of authority to proceed. This can take various forms, such as a key, a staff or, as in this case, a tablet . . .

Single line tablets

Therefore, as we swing round through Saltash station, look out for an iron hoop thing, placed in a holder on top of a short post, set at the right height for the fireman to insert his arm. The speed restriction is 15 mph, so it won't hurt much. Well done, you have it; see there is the tablet in the leather pouch attached to the hoop. This half-mile section is just about the shortest tablet section on record, so there is barely time for a look as we rumble slowly across the bridge. Royal Albert Bridge Signal Box and the points marking the end of a single line are located immediately at the end of the bridge. There is a collecting arm shaped like a cow's horn by the signal box, to collect the tablet as we pass. It is fairly easy at this end, but remember that on a long single line railway with intermediate passing places, you would have been expected to master the art of dropping the tablet for one section and collecting the one for the next in one simultaneous juggling action.

A succession of signal boxes marks our steady progress through the Plymouth suburbs, for a very exact stop at North Road station, with the tender filler precisely opposite the water column. The routine of tank filling occupies a few minutes, while the dining cars are removed from the rear of the train by the station pilot engine. This reduction of load is not only welcome but really essential, for the railway through Devon is not a carbon copy of that through Cornwall, but an exaggerated version of it (see Fig 20). The banks are both longer and steeper. The line climbs out of Plymouth on to the southern flanks of Dartmoor by Hemerdon incline, laid out at the extremely severe grade of 1 in 42. We are maybe a few tons over the rated load for this class of locomotive, but it is a dry night and there should be no difficulty.

On the other hand, to stick on such a grade presents major problems. This normally happens because the wheels have insufficient grip on the rails—and hence race or slip—rather than because insufficient tractive force is available in the cylinders. On many inclines there are vicious devices called catch-points, provided to throw run-away vehicles off the line. Hence, if the train happens to

The iron hoop, placed in a holder on top of a short post, which can hold a single line tablet (*British Rail*)

A collecting arm, shaped like a cow's horn, is there to collect the tablet as we pass (*British Rail*)

20 Gradient profile—
Plymouth to Newton Abbot

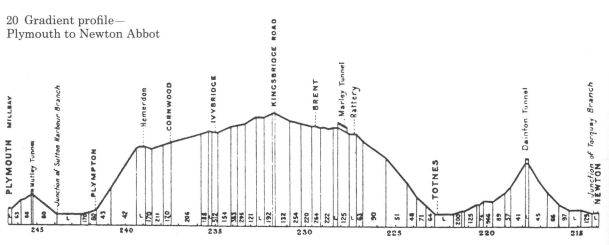

come to rest near one, it is unwise to set back in an attempt to restart. Instantly a whole new chapter of the rule book comes into force and the procedure laid down to obtain assistance is a lengthy one.

Just to illustrate the complications of the driver's job, let's think what the rule book lays down about any involuntary stop out on the line, something which might occur on one in a thousand trips—ie, once every two years or so.

If one has just come to a stand through lack of adhesion then, provided it is certain that the train is not standing on a catch-point (details of the positions of catch-points are provided in the working timetable), one can attempt to restart by first setting back a few yards with rear sanding open. The driving wheels should then be standing in well sanded rails. Then with very careful movement of the throttle, attempt to ease the train into motion. As soon as it starts to move, open the forward sanding gear to maintain the grip as the train proceeds.

Involuntary stops out on the line
If this still does not do the needful, or the cause is something else, then assistance can be summoned either from the rear or from the front. There is also provision for dividing the train and taking the front portion on to the next station, placing it in a siding there and returning for the rest of the train. This measure is not often resorted to in the case of passenger trains.

The fireman should be sent back along the train to meet the guard and explain to him what is wrong. They then must decide whether assistance is best summoned from in front or behind. The guard must in any case then go back and protect his train by placing detonators on the line at prescribed distances, and if assistance is to come from behind, on to the next signal box in rear. If he is to summon assistance from ahead, the fireman must first obtain a Wrong Line Order form from the driver, duly filled in and signed, and take this to the signal box ahead.

There are endless permutations concerning what to do in slightly varying circumstances, say, if either guard or fireman is not available—for example, if the communication cord has been pulled the guard's primary duty is to attend to the passenger who pulled it, in which case the fireman must protect in the rear. Other sorts of circumstances which bring different sub-clauses of the rules into play are fog or falling snow, or two locomotives on the train.

In all, thirty closely printed pages of the rule book deal with this matter. Perhaps one could quote rule 180 (a), to show the tone . . .

'Should the train foul, or be dangerously near to, any line or lines used by trains running in the opposite direction, in addition to the guard going back to protect the train in accordance with rule 179, the Driver of the disabled train must immediately detach his engine, if it be able to travel, and run forward with it not less than $\frac{3}{4}$-mile from the obstruction, where the Fireman must place three detonators, 10 yards apart, on any obstructed line or lines used by trains running in the opposite direction and rejoin his engine.

To be printed on GREEN *paper.*

Form referred to in Rule 183, clause (g).

....................................Railway.

(A supply of these Forms must be kept by each Driver.)

RONG LINE ORDER FORM B.
DRIVER TO SIGNALMAN.

he Signalman at....................*signal box.*

ow an assisting engine or breakdown van to proceed in the wrong direction to my which is stationary on the*...................

t.................. I will not move my engine y direction until the arrival of the assisting e.

points exist at..................

Signed........................*Driver.*

..............19... Time issued.........m.

†Countersigned................................
Signalman.

at........................*signal box.*

t name of line, for example, Up or Down Main, Fast, Slow or Goods.

ecessary.

67

'T' board at end of
temporary speed restriction
(*British Rail*)

In running forward the Driver must sound the engine whistle, exhibit a hand danger signal and, in addition, show a red head light when passing through tunnel, or after sunset or during fog or falling snow, in order to stop any train that may be approaching on the opposite line or lines. Should a train approach on the obstructed line or lines before the detonators have been laid down as prescribed, the Fireman must immediately place 3 detonators on the line or lines affected as far as possible from the obstruction . . .'

The rule goes on to talk about what happens if the engine is disabled; obviously, the fireman goes forward on foot or, if the fireman is disabled, the driver . . . and so on, through thirty pages. Perhaps it should be added that, in spite of these onerous duties laid upon them, the men of the footplate have very rarely been found wanting when the call comes.

Temporary speed restriction

The tank is now full, the guard is giving the right-away and *Forward* makes a clean and snappy start, through Mutley tunnel, then downhill past the loco sheds at Laira. Because of the 15 mph speed restriction at Tavistock tunnel, there is no chance for any sort of a run at the Hemerdon bank. Two yellow lights side-by-side set in a yellow arrow-shaped board, with a '15' illuminated cut-out sign above, warn us of the approach of the restricted length; the actual start and end of it are marked by illuminated 'C' and 'T' signs respectively. We rumble over newly laid unsettled permanent way at this regulation snail's pace, while ahead in the moonlight the grade looks like the roof of a house. Then, with full regulator and cut-off advanced to 45%, the exhaust blasts out of the chimney in the traditional 'square blocks'; the sound of *Forward* wide open like this is one to excite the soul of any steam man. The exhaust injector is full open and the oil latch three-quarters open, a combination that keeps the water level well up and makes enough steam, against the inflow of cooler water, to meet the enormous demands of the cylinders under these conditions of working.

Two more saw-tooth sections of railway bring us to Newton Abbot, junction for the Torquay line, whence a set of six coaches is to be added to our rear, a circumstance which is no cause for concern, since the serious grades are now all behind.

The next section of line is that which winds in and out of tunnels along the sea shore—a pleasure for us, but less so for the engineers whose job it is to take on the destructive powers of Davy Jones. No high speeds are possible but once alongside the Exe estuary speed can rise.

Picking up water at speed

Remarks made earlier indicate how most controls on a steam locomotive are massive, are heavy to turn and need a knack as well, in order to operate them satisfactorily. None are more so than the screw which lowers the water-scoop, which we shall require at Exminster, just ahead. The problem lies in the fact that it is often

Exminster water troughs—note how a short gradient prevents the water flowing out of the ends of the troughs (*British Rail*)

No-one in the first coach should get a wetting (*Brian Hollingsworth*)

necessary to lift the scoop quickly; either because the tender is full and a Niagara Falls effect on the first carriage is better avoided, or because the scoop is lowered below the rails and very often some points or other fittings occur in the four-foot immediately after the end of the troughs. Attempts to scoop these into the tender are equally unsatisfactory. Alas, screws are inherently slow in their action and considerable forward judgement is required.

The troughs themselves have no ends (the water is kept in them by the fact that the railway is laid on a short gradient at either end) and at Exminster there are no immediate obstructions. So start winding the handle down now, watch the tank gauge on the tender and well before the level reaches the top start winding it up again. This is much harder, because the weight of the water in the scoop as well as the scooping effect itself add to the resistance . . . Very reasonable, most of the 1,500 gallons or so used since Plymouth have been replaced and no one in the first coach got a wetting.

The next section of line
winds in and out of tunnels
along the sea-shore
(*Colourviews Picture
Library*)

70

Actaeon

While, after a brief stop at Exeter, *Forward* forges her apparently effortless way up the steady twenty-three mile climb to the summit at Whiteball, we the crew sitting comfortably on cushioned seats in the all-weather cab, one might think for a moment of another locomotive and train, making its way up here a century and a third ago, on the opening day of this railway line from Exeter to Bristol. *Actaeon* did not have a cab, not even a weatherboard; the only protection was some railings round the footplate behind the so-called gothic firebox casing. Daniel Gooch, the young locomotive superintendent, who drove personally, had had a long day; this special train for the guests at the opening banquet left Paddington station in London soon after 7.30 am and now, in the evening of May Day, 1844, had begun the journey home. The 194 miles to London were covered in the then astonishing time of 4 hrs 40 mins, including at least 4 stops for water. This would involve an average speed, when moving, of almost 50 mph, much faster than any running elsewhere at that time by rail or, indeed, any other medium.

Actaeon was a 2–2–2 with inside cylinders, one of sixty-two similar standard locomotives supplied to the GWR to Gooch's design during 1840–42. They were known as the *Fire Fly* class and carried nothing so mundane as a number. In fact, they carried awfully little in the way of accessories at all . . .. Injectors, brakes (other than on the tender), pressure gauges, mechanical lubricators, spring buffers, automatic couplers, train heating, power reversers, firing by other means than by hand, water scoops, electric light, sanding gear and many other 'essentials' were far in the future.

Perhaps not everyone's taste on a winter's night, but imagine how wonderful it must have been on a warm May evening to bowl through the lovely countryside on the open platform of such a delightful fire-chariot. The use of coke as fuel meant almost no smoke and, although the locomotives of those days were by no means as efficient as

Actaeon, built in 1841 by Nasmyth, Gaskell & Co of Manchester for the Great Western Railway
Length (including tender) 38 ft 6 in.
Height 14 ft 10 in.
Width 9 ft 3 in.
Weight 36 tons; on driving axle 11.2 tons
Cylinders 15¾ in. bore × 18 in. stroke
Wheelbase 6 ft 7 in. × 6 ft 7 in.
Driving wheel diameter 7 ft 0 in.
Boiler diameter 48 in.
Heating surface
Grate area 13.5 sq ft
Tractive effort 3,400 lbs
Water capacity 800 gallons
Fuel (coke) capacity 1½ tons

Actaeon bowls along
through open countryside
(*Ink and wash drawing by
George Heiron*)

Forward, the fact that the power output is relatively small—80 tons
would be a heavy train for this little 2–2–2—meant that the task of
firing was not too physically strenuous. It is comforting to see a
familiar glass tube water gauge fixed to the side of the firebox, well
out of the way in case of a burst.

A boiler feed-pump, of course, is pumping all the time we are going
along, but there is a bye-pass valve to return the water back to the
tender if the boiler gets too full. We shall meet the bye-pass
arrangement again in Chapter 11. The only way to check the pressure
on the *Fire Fly* locomotives is to feel the spring balance lever of the
safety valve. If it is easy to lift, then pressure is near to the point at
which the valve is set to blow off, ie, the maximum; if it is hard to lift,
then pressure is low.

Stopping is quite a problem with *Actaeon*. Normal stops can be made
by screwing down the tender handbrakes; extra stopping power can
be summoned up by a blast on the special deep-toned brake whistle—
on hearing this the guard will apply his brake. In the last resort the
locomotive can be reversed. Sanding is done by walking along the
railed running plate to the front of the engine and doing it from there
by hand.

Apart from the reversing lever and regulator, an ordinary whistle
and an ashpan damper make up the rest of the controls. There is no
sign of a blower on any of the photographs or drawings, so presumably
the long chimney provided enough natural draught. Some pictures

DANGER

CAUTION

ALL RIGHT

Early hand-signals (*Author's collection*)

show what appears to be some sort of smokebox damper, presumably to control the draught, worked by a long rod from the driving position.

Lucky Daniel Gooch to have the chance not only to design and have built these excellent early standard locomotives but also to drive one himself to Exeter and back on the opening day. Even though, as he says in his diary, 'It was a very hard day's work for me, as, apart from driving the engine a distance of 390 miles, I had to be out early in the morning to see that all was right for our trip, and while at Exeter was busy with matters connected with the opening, so that my only chance of sitting down was the hour we were at dinner. Next day my back ached so much I could hardly walk.' Truly there were giants in those days. However, in compensation, 'Mr Brunel wrote me a very handsome letter, thanking me for what I had done . . . .'.

Victorian signal

The signalling arrangements of 1844 display a refreshing simplicity, corresponding to that of the locomotive. They are the responsibility of railway policemen—a hundred and more years on, signalmen will still be called 'bobbies'—who show a danger signal for three minutes after any train has passed and a caution signal for another seven minutes after that. 'Danger' or 'Stop' is indicated at night by a red light; in the day-time by a high cross-bar signal or by the policeman raising both arms above his head, as still used today. For all-clear the light displayed at night was white, not green as it is today, whilst the crossbar signal is turned through a right-angle, displaying a disc which, previously being seen sideways on, had been invisible. The crossbar then becomes invisible in its turn. An arm extended horizontally is the corresponding hand signal.

Caution signals take the form of fan-tails, pointing away from the line for caution or, at night, a *green* light or, by hand, one arm raised. In an uncomplicated landscape the station signals could be seen a mile or two out. So much for how to drive an engine in the early days of steam.

In a flash the scene changes and we are again confined in *Forward's* comfortable and superbly equipped cab; at the same time realising something of what was in the old enginemen's minds when they threatened industrial action against the company's decision to provide them with shelter against the weather. With sixteen times the load of *Actaeon, Forward,* with oil latch wide open and full regulator, is burning 7 gallons of oil and evaporating 64 gallons of water each minute, is developing 3000 horse-power in the cylinders and managing to hold 53 mph on this 1 in 155 gradient. The final two miles, at 1 in 115, bring her down to 44 mph as we enter Whitehall tunnel and begin the descent of Wellington bank.

How not to run a railway

Wellington bank! Great Western history was written here when on 9th May 1904 a 4–4–0 called *City of Truro* came down this winding

A disc and cross-bar signal surviving—in poor condition—until recent times (*British Rail*)

descent with an ocean liner special at a speed certainly exceeding 100 mph. A maximum of 104.2 mph was claimed as a world record for many years, although a recent analysis of the timings showed that this was possibly a little high. The real achievement lay in the fact that *City of Truro* made the run from Plymouth to Bristol in 124 minutes for the 127 miles—66 minutes under our fast schedule and 36 under the timing we are attempting in order to try for a punctual arrival at Bristol. The run was characterised by a blatant disregard of speed restrictions. *City of Truro* has (using the present tense—she survives in retirement at Swindon museum) 6 ft 8½ in. wheels but our 4 ft 11 in. ones limit us to 75 mph or so. In any case this incident creeps in here as an example of how not to drive a locomotive and perhaps also, how not to run a railway. Be that as it may, the Great Western kept the details secret for several years. Kipling puts it in perspective

'Now these are the laws of the Jungle
and many and mighty are they
But the head and the hoof of the Law
and the haunch and the hump is—Obey!'

At the foot of the bank stands Taunton where we cross from the main London line to the parallel Bristol line. Then Cogload water troughs and a fast straight run the remainder of the way to the outskirts of Bristol. This forty-five miles of level running is different to any we have done so far. Throttle wide open, cut-off wound back to 17%, oil latch about two thirds open, exhaust injector set to keep water level constant and at a steady 70 mph the minutes, the miles and the green signal lights fly past. Perfect.

Fog!

A wisp of vapour steals across the flat marshy fields, then another and another—suddenly the outside world is a white wall of fog, the driver's special nightmare. At our speed there is no hope of seeing signals; but our 'little friend in the corner' is a friend in need and its comforting rings give us confidence to keep up an unslackening pace. Pity engine drivers in the days before AWS—they were nearly as badly off as motorway drivers today. At least the old ones had detonators placed on the line by fogmen upon which to rely.

The siren suddenly sounds but this time no haughty stroke of the 'cancel' handle. Instead, a thankful one as I opt to control the brake application myself rather than allow the automatic application to run its course; next, the routine of shutting off steam and oil fuel and making a service application. This is the moment when the inexperienced would-be or trainee driver definitely has to bow out. Effectively blindfolded, the man in charge must not only know exactly where he is—by the sound of bank or cutting, over-bridge or underbridge, points or platform—but also what is the exact configuration of the railway ahead. At walking pace we creep forward; yes, there's the bridge over the marsh dyke. Twenty rail-joints (remember them, diddley-dum and all that?) beyond is Uphill

75

and Bleadon outer home and there is a glimmer of green at the head of the post. OK, now we creep on to find the home—the starter at the end of the platform is easy. Both these signals turn out to be at clear. Now we can open up again—but gone is any hope of regaining lost time. As the distance flies by, the fog persists but so do all-clear rings.

The approach to Bristol is heralded by a change from semaphore signals to colour-light and, for us, from invisible to visible ones. As the first one blazes out at us from the murk, any nostalgia for the good old days is overlaid with thankfulness for the benefits of present ones; these welcome lights take us by the hand and lead us gently to rest alongside the great main platform of Temple Meads station. The Grand Junction Express is 15 minutes late.

If it should be true that dreams reflect some process of rearranging the contents of the memory, it is not surprising that what appears next is not Grand Junction, Birmingham (and the start of the Grand Junction Railway over which London was first joined to Liverpool and Manchester) but Grand Junction, Colorado, USA, a mile high up in the Rockies.

Approaching Bristol
(*British Rail*)

7

BLACK FIVE IN COLORADO

RAILROADING WITHOUT SIGNALS

'Extra 5428 West is ready to go—she's standing on the Ought Track—here's your orders' were the words that introduced us to a whole new world of railroading. The 'Ought Track' turned out to be the No. 0 independent line between the Westbound Main and the No. 1 yard siding, while locomotive No. 5428 (extra trains take their number from the locomotive) was a typical British coal-burning 4–6–0 a 'ten-wheeler' she'd be called in America—of the competent and legendary type known as *Black Five* (see Fig 21).

5428's cab is spartan compared to *Forward*'s—no luxuries like electric light, power reverse or nicely padded bucket seats, for example—and only half the number of controls, valves and gauges. Although most are differently placed or arrayed, the essential functions remain the same. Some things are the other way round; the train brakes are vacuum instead of air, for example, and the driving position is on the left instead of the right.

Train orders
A quick inspection shows *5428* to be indeed ready to go; fire in good shape, no serious leakages, lubricators full and plenty of fuel and water. The train is a through freight, a 'hot-shot' as it would be called on the American side of the Atlantic; happily we have been spared the nightmare of running that exclusively British horror, the unbraked or partially braked goods train. On the other hand we are going to run the one we have on a busy single line railroad operated according to the traditional steam-age North American operating rules. The main shock is that we shall now be avoiding collisions with other trains not by fixed signals but instead by the timetable—see Fig 22. This will be modified by instructions—known as train orders—received from the boss of the line, a gentleman known as the 'despatcher', in whose infallibility it is necessary to have an almost religious faith.

It will be our judgement that will keep our train clear of other trains that are superior as defined in the rules. This would typically mean taking to a siding when one is due; no signalman of course—one of us gets down and throws the switch and we go inside. So that

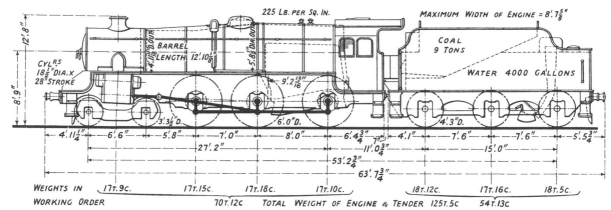

225 LB. PER SQ. IN.

MAXIMUM WIDTH OF ENGINE = 8'.7⅝"

COAL 9 TONS

WATER 4000 GALLONS

BARREL LENGTH 12'.10⅝"

CYL.RS 18½"DIA.X 28"STROKE

WEIGHTS IN WORKING ORDER — 17T.9C. | 17T.15C. | 17T.18C. | 17T.10C. | 18T.12C. | 17T.16C. | 18T.5C.

70T.12C   TOTAL WEIGHT OF ENGINE & TENDER 125T.5C   54T.13C

21 Diagram of *Black Five* with principal weights and dimensions

Heating surface, tubes large and small 1,478.7 sq ft firebox 171.3 sq ft
Total evaporative 1,650 sq ft
Superheater 359.3 sq ft

Combined heating surfaces 2,009.3 sq ft
Superheater elements 28, 1¼ in. dia. outs
Large tubes 28, 5⅛ in. dia. outs

Small tubes 151, 1⅞ in. dia. outs
(13 ft 2⅞ in. in between tubeplates)
Grate area 28.65 sq ft
Tractive effort 25,455 lb

22 An example of an American railroad timetable sheet—all extra trains must keep clear of the booked ones shown (*Author's collection*)

inferior trains do not collide with us, it also means not running ahead of time and that in its turn means having our watches accurate.

Because of the necessity for order, we find that, just as in the unjust human world, one train is superior to another by class; that is, passenger trains have rights over through freights, hot-shots over locals, regular over extra trains and so on. Trains that are equal by class have their superiority governed by direction; in this case

THIRD DIVISION—THIRD DISTRICT—Mears Jct. and Alamosa

WESTWARD			Distance from Denver	Time Table No. 99 July 20, 1919	Dist. from Alamosa		EASTWARD	
SECOND CLASS		FIRST CLASS					FIRST CLASS	SECOND CLASS
323 Mixed		317 Denver, Alamosa and Durango Passenger				Siding Capacity in cars	318 Denver, Alamosa and Durango Passenger	324 Mixed
Leave Monday and Friday		Leave Daily Except Sunday		STATIONS		Passing Tracks	Arrive Daily Except Sunday	Arrive Tuesday and Saturday
			215.11	S **SALIDA** N 10.91	85.33	Yard		
9.40AM		4.50PM	226.02	**MEARS JUNC.** RWCY 3.56	74.42	32	11.26AM	3.31PM
10.20		f 5.15	229.57	PONCHA PASS Y 3.26	70.87	36	f 11.21	3.01
10.49 318		f 5.27	232.83	ROUND HILL WY 6.16	67.61	50	f 10.49 323	1.40
11.11		f 5.42	238.99	LINTON 6.35	61.45	46	f 10.31	1.02
11.36		s 5.57	245.34	Vg **VILLA GROVE** RDWCY 5.59	55.10	45	s 10.13	12.41
12.08PM		f 6.12	250.93	MINERAL HOT SPRINGS 6.08	49.51	49	f 9.57	12.01PM
12.45		f 6.27	257.01	MIRAGE 5.68	43.43	49	f 9.43	11.36
1.15 3.00		s 6.44	262.69	Mf **MOFFAT** DWY 6.21	37.75	103	s 9.30	11.06
3.25		f 7.00	268.90	LA GARITA 5.40	31.54	49	f 9.13	10.33
3.47		f 7.12	274.30	GIBSON 5.97	26.14	49	f 8.55	10.08
4.12		s 7.26	280.27	Gr **HOOPER** D 6.57	20.17	49	f 8.39	9.33
4.34		f 7.41	286.84	MOSCA 7.27	13.60	49	f 8.25	9.07
5.00		f 7.59	294.11	McGINTY 6.33	6.33	39	f 8.09	8.38
5.45PM		8.20PM	300.44	As-Rm **ALAMOSA** RNWCYTS		Yard	7.50AM	8.00AM
Arrive Monday and Friday		Arrive Daily Except Sunday		(85.33)			Leave Daily Except Sunday	Leave Tuesday and Saturday
(8.25) 8.84		(3.30) 21.78		......Time Over District...... ......Average Miles per Hour......			(3. 6) 22.90	(7.31) 9.90

SPECIAL INSTRUCTIONS.

C-1. EASTWARD TRAINS ARE SUPERIOR TO WESTWARD TRAINS OF THE SAME CLASS.
C-2. The west wye switch at Alamosa is set and locked for La Veta line. Third Division trains will come to full stop before entering Alamosa yard.
C-3. Passenger trains will not exceed a speed of fifteen miles per hour and freight trains ten miles per hour down grade between Poncha Pass and Mears Junction and Poncha Pass and Round Hill.
C-4. Alder, at MP 236.9 is mail station for Nos. 317 and 318.

5428, a typical British coal-burning 4–6–0 (*Brian Hollingsworth*)

Westbound is superior to Eastbound. All these superiority rules can be over-ruled or reversed by specific train orders issued by the despatcher. Perhaps one should add that this rather primitive American system has, in the diesel age, the same status as the unbraked freight in Britain; that is, still with us but on the way out for important lines.

That exclusively British horror, the unbraked or partially braked goods train (*Author's collection*)

Coal firing—breaking up
lumps on the tender
(*Colourviews Limited*)

Right:
The gentle art of coal
firing—placing coal in the
front corners of the box
(*Colourviews Limited*)

Coal firing

Anyway, one thing we have to learn is the gentle art of firing a coal-burning engine. With oil, when fuel is sprayed into the firebox it burns away immediately. With coal, however, it need not necessarily be burnt immediately and can remain alight but quiescent for some time; becoming drawn up into a blazing white heat if the engine is opened up and worked harder. This is a great advantage in overcoming peaks and troughs in the demand for steam, but it does mean having to think well ahead.

The main disadvantage of coal-burning, as far as the crew is concerned, is the really heavy manual labour of filling a shovel with coal from the tender, turning the shovel round and throwing the coal to the appropriate place in the firebox, a distance which in our case can be as much as 8 ft. In average terms, we are talking of consumption approaching a ton an hour on this journey, or rather more than three shovelfuls a minute. A fireman will spend almost half his time shovelling, putting a 'round' of six or eight shovelfuls in the box every couple of minutes or so when steam is on.

The classic rule for hand-firing is 'little and often' and the objective is to maintain an even fire. Too thick and the air needed for the coal to burn cannot get through; too thin and there is a danger of a hole developing in the fire and cold air spoiling steam generation, as well as maybe causing leaks in the firebox.

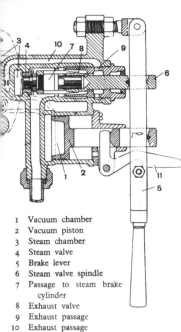

1 Vacuum chamber
2 Vacuum piston
3 Steam chamber
4 Steam valve
5 Brake lever
6 Steam valve spindle
7 Passage to steam brake cylinder
8 Exhaust valve
9 Exhaust passage
10 Exhaust passage
11 Trigger

23 Combined vacuum and steam brake valve (*Author's collection*)

24 Combined vacuum and steam brake—*Black Five* is equipped with a similar arrangement (*Author's collection*)

A mechanical system of stoking was applied to many American steam locomotives, but to no (or virtually no) British ones for home use. Other people such as foreigners or colonials got them but the indigenous breed of engineman had no need, it was felt, of such molly-coddling devices. Operation of a mechanical stoker is a matter of running the donkey engine which drives the feed screw at the right pace and adjusting the steam jets which distribute the coal over the firebed.

On a coal-fired locomotive the state of the fire—whence comes all the power—is of paramount importance. Amongst the problems is what is called clinker; impurities in the coal can fuse together and form clinker on the fire-bars. This can prevent the fire burning properly. It may be present even when, looked at superficially, the fire seems excellent. Another possible thing to watch out for is the state of the ash-pan, which is provided under the grate to catch the ashes. If it has become full and hence is choking the grate, satisfactory steaming may be impossible. However, a quick inspection and conversation with the crew handing over indicates that all is well.

Vacuum brakes

A quick oil round and then it is time for a thought regarding the new braking system. The actual operation of this brake is very similar to the air-brake on *Forward*. The combined vacuum (for the train) and steam (for the loco and tender) application valve is handled in very much the same manner (see Fig 23), although it works in a vertical rather than a horizontal plane. In the vacuum world you do, however, talk of inches of mercury as in a barometer, rather than air pressure in lbs per sq. in. Again, a typical brake application involves a reduction of 8 to 10 units, ie, from say 21 in. to 12 in.

Vacuum is created by steam jet in the small and in the large ejectors, devices that are very much simpler than steam-driven air

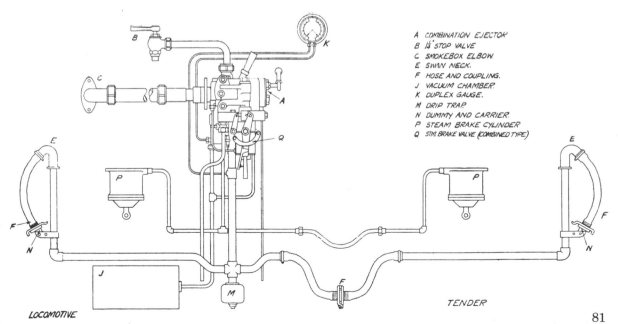

A COMBINATION EJECTOR
B 1¼" STOP VALVE
C SMOKEBOX ELBOW.
E SWAN NECK.
F HOSE AND COUPLING.
J VACUUM CHAMBER.
K DUPLEX GAUGE.
M DRIP TRAP.
N DUMMY AND CARRIER.
P STEAM BRAKE CYLINDER
Q STM. BRAKE VALVE (COMBINED TYPE)

LOCOMOTIVE

TENDER

25 An actual train order—note grimy finger prints! (*Author's collection*)

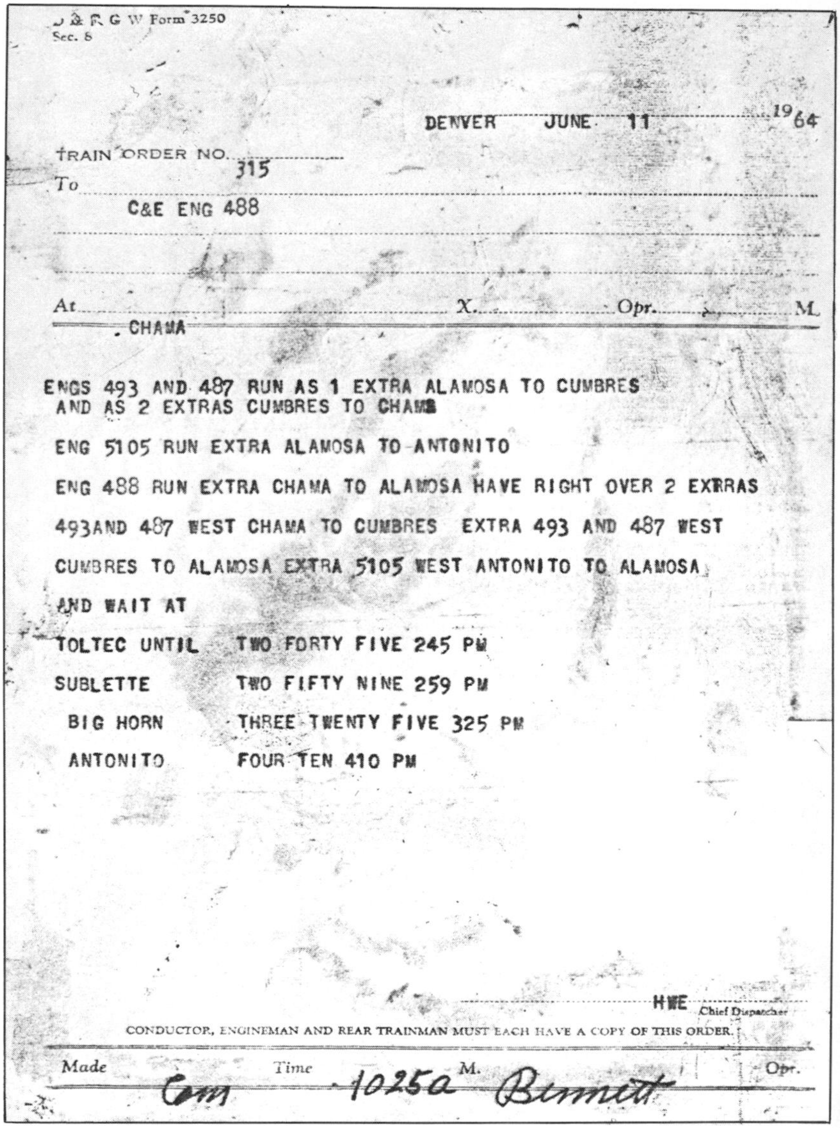

D & R G W Form 3250
Sec. 8

DENVER JUNE 11 1964

TRAIN ORDER NO. 315

To C&E ENG 488

At CHAMA X. Opr. M.

ENGS 493 AND 487 RUN AS 1 EXTRA ALAMOSA TO CUMBRES AND AS 2 EXTRAS CUMBRES TO CHAMA

ENG 5105 RUN EXTRA ALAMOSA TO ANTONITO

ENG 488 RUN EXTRA CHAMA TO ALAMOSA HAVE RIGHT OVER 2 EXTRAS 493AND 487 WEST CHAMA TO CUMBRES EXTRA 493 AND 487 WEST CUMBRES TO ALAMOSA EXTRA 5105 WEST ANTONITO TO ALAMOSA AND WAIT AT

TOLTEC UNTIL	TWO FORTY FIVE 245 PM
SUBLETTE	TWO FIFTY NINE 259 PM
BIG HORN	THREE TWENTY FIVE 325 PM
ANTONITO	FOUR TEN 410 PM

HWE Chief Dispatcher

CONDUCTOR, ENGINEMAN AND REAR TRAINMAN MUST EACH HAVE A COPY OF THIS ORDER.

Made Com Time 1025a M. Bennett Opr.

compressors. The small ejector is normally left on and is intended to maintain the vacuum against leakages etc, whilst the large one is used to actually create vacuum in the system. This is normally done when the brakes are released. The system is so designed that, if all is well, there is a full 21 in. of vacuum in the train pipe when the brakes are off. If this vacuum is destroyed, the brakes are then applied in proportion to the amount of air that is admitted. The steam brake on the locomotive is applied in proportion by a so-called proportional valve. All we have to do is to note that the correct vacuum of 21 in. is held; the train being held by the hand parking brake on the tender.

Meet the conductor

The guard—perhaps we should now begin calling him the conductor—is on his way down. He'll give us details of our 'consist'

By law, all North American locomotives carry bells, sounded continuously while moving in yards and depots (*Brian Hollingsworth*)

(he means the number and details of the cars forming the train) and it is necessary to have a clear understanding with him of the significance of the orders we have received and the meets with regular and other trains. Comparing watches is another thing to be done. Note that both fireman and driver must participate and that it is the fireman's duty when a mile or so away from a siding at which a meet is to be made to remind his mate of the fact. It is also necessary before we leave to ascertain from the despatcher's office here that all superior trains due have arrived or left and to receive clearance to go by signing a clearance card.

Our orders (see Fig 25) give us a schedule of times at intermediate points on our 100 mile journey. As a westbound extra we would normally be inferior to all regular trains; the only ones we would be superior to are eastbound extras. However, there is another order giving us rights over the westbound and eastbound local freights, which pick up and set out cars at every nook and cranny along the road. Inevitably these attract such a name as *Cannonball,* a sarcastic reference to the speed with which they make progress. Both *Cannonballs* will have received copies of the orders and it will be their job to get clear of us.

An unsignalled railway

Armed in this way, we prepare to venture out on to this unsignalled passenger railway, a traumatic experience indeed for anyone from the Old World. The British equivalent would have not only switches and signals controlled by signalmen at all places where trains might be crossed or passed, but in addition no train would enter a single line section without a physical token of authority to do so, as described in Chapter 6. It is strange to reflect that American locomotives have always had every refinement available at the time for making life easy for the engineman, whilst British ones lagged behind. At the same time British signalling made life out of all proportion easier for the enginemen there. In recent years, of course, progress in electric

British loco *King George V* complete with bell for operation in the USA (*Author's collection*)

Can there be any pleasure greater than handling a well-found steam engine through lovely country in glorious weather? (*Brian Hollingsworth*)

HI-BALL

Given by waving the hand from A to B as illustrated. Sometimes used in place of Standard PROCEED signal when a train is leaving.

A frequent and peculiarly American horror, the unguarded public level crossing (*E. J. Gulash*)

signalling on single lines has brought the two countries closer together. Token working is no longer universal in Britain and unsignalled train-order territory is contracting in America.

Highball!

Like each of the four British locomotives which have in recent years run in America (*King George V, Royal Scot, Coronation* and *Flying Scotsman*), *5428* should strictly need both headlight and a bell. The headlight we won't need on a day-time ride and the sounding of a vacuum-operated bell, which is required to be rung continuously while moving in yards and depôts, will be our first action on receiving the conductor's highball—we call it a right-away. Another matter which has to be taken care of is a double long blast on the whistle, according to the rather complex code of whistles specified in the standard rules. (In Britain the code of whistle calls is purely a local matter, usually specifying some direction of travel.)

With the reversing screw in full forward gear, open cylinder-cocks (hand-operated, of course), you release the hand brake and I lift the regulator handle. With a few clanks but a lovely strong sharp beat *5428* gets hold of her train and eases it out of the Ought Track at Grand Junction through the switches and crossings on to the branch. Now close the blower, start an injector and put the first round into the box. Once clear of the yard the bell is no longer sounded and the cut-off reduced as speed increases.

This cut-off business has quite a mystique of its own, as we found out on *Forward*. But unlike *Forward, 5428* has covered a lot of miles since last in shops and this introduces another factor into consideration. Whilst it is true that it is most economical when running at speed to fling in all the steam needed during the first 15% of the stroke, it is also true that it is easier on the bearings to put it in at a lower rate and take longer—say during the first 25%. In other words, regulator not quite so wide open and the cut-off brought back only as far as the mechanism will accept to 'kicking point' as it is sometimes called. Maybe we shall have to work a trifle harder with the shovel, but at the same time our teeth will not be shaken out of our heads.

It remains to mention two other items: the first present but useless and the other absent but useful—until we have learned to get along without it. In unsignalled territory the automatic warning system, 'our little friend in the corner' has no function. At the same time we will have to keep to the speed limits so precisely specified in the timetable by feel or judgement rather than with a glance at the speedometer.

Can there be any pleasure greater than handling a well-found steam engine through lovely country in glorious weather? In the best traditions of such great enginemen as Bill Hoole of King's Cross, fireman and driver will both take turns at the firing, so perhaps it will not be too onerous for either of us. *5428* rattles and rolls a bit, but not so bad that one cannot quickly acquire the knack of keeping one's balance with both hands on the shovel. At least there are doors filling the gap between cab and tender; on so many British locomotives there is a wide and disconcerting void instead.

Unguarded grade crossings

The first taste of the new world comes as a sign 'W' announces the imminence of a frequent and particularly American railroad horror (easily matching the British unbraked freight train)—the unguarded public road grade crossing. Two longs followed by two shorts is the specified call and we sound it loud and prolonged with our fabulous American whistle until the eagles for miles around leave their nests in alarm. Hopefully the deafest of truck drivers will hear and take note. A sigh of relief as we are safe across—with only another forty-five grade crossings to come today.

Meet No. 22

The place for our first meet is now approaching. The train order we received reads 'NO. 22 MEET EXTRA 5428 WEST AT BIG HORN'.

You as the fireman should have read it aloud to me on receipt and now that the time has come (by strict rule at $1\frac{1}{4}$ miles from the meet point), I expect a reminder from you in the words 'We meet No. 22 at this station'. One mile from the siding we pass a warning sign 'S'. This is a sign for me to close the regulator and run at strict caution, while you react by opening the blower a touch, putting on the second injector to prevent her wasting steam through the safety valves and adjusting the damper to damp down the fire in case of a long stand. At the same time I sound two longs and a short (according to rule) on the whistle, which lets the conductor know that we have remembered; otherwise he would be expected to take emergency action—he has a brake valve in his caboose—to stop the train.

A gentle brake application (10 in. of vacuum) brings us to a stand just clear of the switch leading into the siding. The switch stand which controls it is fixed alongside. It is your task to get down and throw or open the switch, so that we can run inside, which we do, stopping with the whole train clear of the main line. Once this is done, the conductor or his flagman at the rear of the train will get down and line up for the main, the switch we have just passed over. Incidentally, with a typical North American mile-long freight it would be necessary for the caboose to report the train clear inside by radio to the locomotive. There is nothing to do now but wait.

No. 22 passenger is heard coming long before she comes into view and soon the varnish roars by, green flags fluttering from the pilot beam of the locomotive, a whooo-ooo, whoo, whoo from its whistle. A long and two shorts and we quickly answer with two shorts. If we had not responded, No. 22 would have made an emergency stop and (no doubt acrimoniously) asked us to explain. The reason is that the green flags and the whistle signal signify that No. 22 is running in two portions today as First 22 and Second 22. You will appreciate that it is fairly important that we should not pull out before Second 22 has gone by. At best it would mean what is called a 'cornfield' meet—at worst a head-on collision. It should be added that identification

numbers 1–22 and 2–22 are displayed at the front of each of these respective trains.

Fifteen minutes later Second 22 goes by—this time there are no green flags to indicate a third portion following and so, with two long blasts, we pull out on to the main. We halt to allow the rear crew to line up the switch for the main as before and set off. *5428* may be long out of shops but she has a lovely sharp even beat—a pleasure to listen to as we gather speed. The routine of taking turn and turn about with the firing occupies us for a while. A station comes into view. Checking watches tells us we are running right up to but not ahead of our schedule as the depôt flashes by with its order signals in the vertical (negative) position; no orders for *5428*. As time goes by *Cannonball* is in our minds, she can't be too far ahead as we are closing in on her schedule. The train order 'EXTRA 5428 HAS RIGHTS OVER NO. 487 BIG HORN TO HERMOSA' absolves us of responsibility, but it is no use being in the right when they are lifting the engine with the big hook to see if you are underneath.

Catching up the Cannonball

In the course of rounding a series of bends we come upon a fusee smoking in the middle of the track. A fusee is a kind of all-weather firework which burns for 10 minutes and can be seen both by day and night. It provides a crude but effective indication that *487* is less than that time ahead of us. Clearly *487* has underestimated her time into Wilderness Siding three miles ahead; although she may well now be inside and clear, it is our duty to wait for the fusee to burn out, then run at caution. In fact, as Wilderness comes into view this proves to be the case and with one long whoooo-ooo . . . we run through on the main.

A drink of water

By now *5428* has been running an hour and each of us has put half a ton of coal (out of the five we had with us) into that firebox. At the same time 2,200 of the 3,000 gallons of water originally in our tender has vanished up the chimney, and it is therefore fortunate that the tank at Cresco lies not far ahead. Practice enables us to make a precise stop, spotting the tank filling hole opposite the delivery pipe. There is actually a rule which says that the locomotives of freight trains must uncouple and draw ahead to take water, 'except as otherwise provided'. This has to do with the problems of halting with exactitude long trains with the feet of slack inevitable with the American buck-eye pattern coupler; and therefore nothing to do with our shortish train and screw couplings.

The hinged delivery pipe—more a delivery chute—is very convenient and soon a torrent of water is filling the tender. It is even a one man job, for the valve can be operated by double strings from the top of the tender. In the meantime our conductor is arranging to protect our train from the rear, sending the flagman back 'a sufficient distance to ensure full protection'. The flagman will place two torpedos (detonators) on the rail and wait our air recall. There is now

TAKE WATER

Given by closing the hand with the thumb sticking out like a spout, then raising the spout to the lips as though drinking.

On American water tanks,
the hinged delivery pipe is
very convenient (*Brian
Hollingsworth*)

an opportunity to have a look round the engine, putting in a drop of
oil here and there, while feeling and sniffing for any sign of over-
heating. It is true that Black Fives—like Rolls-Royces—never run hot,
but . . .

With the tender full again and the engine OK, it is time to roll five
long blasts to recall the flagman—if we had had to protect from the
front (west) as well the recall signal for that flagman would be four
blasts, enabling protection to be withdrawn separately. Then two
more long ones to indicate 'proceed' and away we go.

Order on the fly

The next little conundrum is No. 24 passenger. Having no orders
concerning this train, it is our responsibility to keep clear of No. 24's
schedule. The rule is that, for passenger trains, opposing inferior
trains should clear their schedule by ten minutes. The timetable
shows No. 24 due at a station called Sublette three miles ahead in 45
minutes time; there is another twelve miles ahead where No. 24 is due
in 30 minutes. To be inside there with ten minutes spare would be
close biting on a sharply curved section of road where high speed is
out of the question; so we settle for the earlier meeting place.

In the meantime Ridgeway station is coming up and we observe the
order signal in the diagonal or half-way position. This means there is
a non-restrictive train order which will be handed up to be caught on
the fly. This is done with a Y-shaped baton, between the prongs of
which is stretched a double strand of string. The order paper is placed

between the strands and held there by twisting them—not too tightly, of course, so that it won't be torn as it is plucked from the device as we go by—an action that should be performed as nonchalantly as taking a newspaper from a passer-by in the street, however fast the train may be moving. With my gauntlet gloves I gather the flimsy from the agent, who then prepares to offer a second copy to our conductor at the rear.

Incidentally, as American enginemen we find ourselves dressed quite differently from the British, with their peaked shiny-top cap and blue overalls. The American hogger sported a blue-and-white striped peaked cap of quite a different shape, often with a bright checked 'thousand-miler' shirt—so called because it is traditionally expected to last 1,000 miles between washes—and the gauntlets mentioned. Eh, what's that? Oh, the order . . . well, it reads 'NO. 24 RUNS 70 MINS LATE HERMOSA TO RIDGEWAY AND 50 MINS LATE RIDGEWAY TO GRAND JUNCTION'. This covers a situation where No. 24 has been delayed; if the despatcher had done nothing all other trains on the road would have been tied up between the scheduled and the actual running time of No. 24. As it is we can set out and make the meet at a place called Rico, twenty miles nearer our destination and 40 minutes earlier; this is worked out with the help of the conductor.

It is mostly a gentle down grade to Rico. *5428* will drift with a breath of steam and the fire will not need more coal for a while—so, time for lunch. Delicious steaks, bacon and eggs can be cooked on a scoured shovel in the firebox; this is, perhaps, for graduate enginemen doing the run for the hundredth time—we will be content with tea and sandwiches.

8

HOME ALONG THE RANGE

WAKING UP

At Rico an engineless freight occupies the siding at the east end. We deduce (correctly as it turns out) that the problem with No. 24 has been the failure of one of 'they new-fangled diseasels' and the locomotive from the freight has been sent back to assist. It presents us with a problem in that the spare room in the siding is at the other end. Fortunately there are still ten minutes until we have to be in the clear and there is time to run through on the main and set back into the siding. Movements of this kind are occasions on which one misses a powered reversing gear. Also, to run forward at this point we need protection; in the absence of a front-end flagman it is your job to walk ahead 'sufficient distance to ensure full protection' and to place detonators on the line. When the train is backed in clear and the switch lined up for the main, you will hear my recall signal of four long blasts.

Climbing up

Right on its new schedule No. 24 runs by and we now face the long climb to Palmer Pass with its thirty miles at 1.5%. Speed soon falls to 20 mph or less in spite of a wide open regulator and late cut-off. Each firing round now consists of twelve shovelfuls instead of eight and the rounds have to follow one another so closely that for practical purposes firing continues without a pause. One injector is on continuously . . . .

For half an hour all goes well. The pressure gauge remains steady and *5428* steams superbly making, in fact, the most wonderful exhaust music as she pounds up the grade. Then, little by little, a combination of factors causes the rot to set in. First, our inexperience combined with increasing tiredness has led to an uneven fire—too thin at the front where it is pulling into holes and too thick at the back where it's nearly out; second, the excellent beginner-proof coal used earlier is now becoming more and more mixed with the inferior grade underneath it in the bunker; third, as a result of the poor coal the fire and ashpan beneath it is getting clogged with ash and clinker. Efforts made with a pricker and dart have made some difference, but have of course interfered with the firing rate. Although the injector

Facing page:
5428 makes wonderful exhaust music as she storms up the grade (*J. P. R. Hunt*)

90

5428 climbing (*Rodney Wildsmith*)

has been turned off, thereby mortgaging the boiler level, pressure is now falling to a point where the vacuum ejector is becoming less effective; since the ejector is in effect holding off the brakes it begins to be a case of 'from whom that hath not shall be taken away even that which he hath'. Soon enough, therefore, the brakes will begin to drag and that will be that.

Out of steam

It seems reasonable to pre-empt this point by stopping at a place of our own choosing; this length of straight track on a slightly easier grade will do . . . .

The blower is put on and we commence the hot, dusty and unpleasant task of cleaning the fire, sorting out some decent coal from amongst the dust and rubbish and bringing it forward from the back of the tender. Clinker is dragged out through the firedoor and thrown over the side. Most American steam locomotives for many years before the end had wide fireboxes, less prone to this kind of trouble, and rockable elements in the grate, which made the problem easier to solve should it occur. Of course, British designers in pre-1939 days were spoilt by the excellent quality of the coal which British engines might expect as their normal diet. On stopping we have whistled a long and three shorts to call for protection in rear; to the front our schedule is sufficient protection. Naturally, the conductor, once he has sent out the flagman, comes along to learn what he has not already guessed about the trouble. With faces red—both literally and figuratively—we tell him.

After 25 minutes patient struggling the fire is again in reasonable shape, the boiler full and the pressure close to blowing-off point; it is time to move off. A little sand to get a grip plus careful handling of the regulator makes easy meat of the start on this heavy gradient. Soon enough *5428* is once more pounding her way up the hillside as if nothing had happened. This time there is one other thing to bear in mind. The summit point—to our fore-shortened gaze from the cab—is like the gable of a house; this means that, as we go over the top, the water-level in the gauge glasses will fall dramatically. Provision for this means having the water level above normal, in fact just out of sight in the top nut, as the summit approaches; yet, as it is, there is barely sufficient energy in hand to keep water and pressure at their present levels.

The thing to do is to put both injectors full on just before the summit is reached. With nice judgement, just enough pressure will remain to take us up the last length of climb; at the same time, taking advantage of the short length of level at the summit, enough water will have been put into the boiler to avoid a dangerously low water level as we begin the descent. A factor in wishing to avoid an ignominious halt is that it would be under the critical eyes of the crew of an eastbound extra waiting for us in the siding. Incidentally, the twists of the line in these hills are such that he is actually travelling due west and we due east, but by the rules we are westbound and therefore westbound we remain.

Braking

As the long descent begins we can again thank our lucky stars that the train is a shortish, tightly screw-coupled British freight and not a typical immense American one, whose automatic couplers each have, as has been mentioned, several inches of 'slack' when connected up. A 150-car train might have 50 ft of slack in all. Such a train would come over the top with the slack pulled out, but once over and running free the cars, unless discouraged, would begin to bunch against the locomotive. If the brake was then firmly applied down the train, the cars would cease to run free and the slack would be pulled out again. Then, if the application was unskillfully made, perhaps too fierce or too sudden, this slack would run out violently and maybe pull out a drawbar. At best this would bring the two parts of the train to a protracted halt; at worst, railroad cars would be scattered like confetti around the surrounding scenery. The problem is greatly accentuated if the grades vary or reverse and, even more involved, on a long down grade the brake reservoirs of the cars will in time exhaust themselves, causing complete loss of brake power. It is therefore necessary to release and re-charge the brakes from time to time—cyclic braking, it is called. In such a case, some of the cars will have their retaining valve turned up manually before starting the descent; this prevents the brakes releasing during the re-charging process, but, of course, they do remain permanently on until manually re-set. The whole process is not at all suitable for tenderfeet such as ourselves.

The vacuum brakes on Extra *5428* West may also need to be re-cycled in a similar but less fraught way. The vacuum on the upper side of the brake piston, on the lower side of and against which the less-than-full-vacuum pressure acts to apply the brakes, can leak back to atmospheric pressure in time. This will gradually reduce the effectiveness of the brakes, but it can similarly be countered by a successive release and application. However, the nightmare of 50 ft of slack action charging up and down the train, causing dire in-train collisions, is not present. This is not to suggest any general superiority of screw-couplings and vacuum brakes over automatic and air—quite the contrary. Really long economic trains could hardly be worked at all with the former combination.

As we roll on down the hill with the fire quiescent, swinging round the curves with an easy motion, perhaps just one thought for those who made it so. The Road-master's situation is well summed up in the jingle . . .

'I am not allowed to run the train, the whistle I can't blow,
    I am not allowed to say how far the railroad cars can go,
I am not allowed to shoot off steam, or even clang a bell,
    But let it jump the goddam track then see who catches hell.'

Anon

Block territory

But *5428* holds the rails smoothly all the way on down to Mears Junction, whence the route continues in automatic block territory with colour-light signalling. In British practice, colour-light running

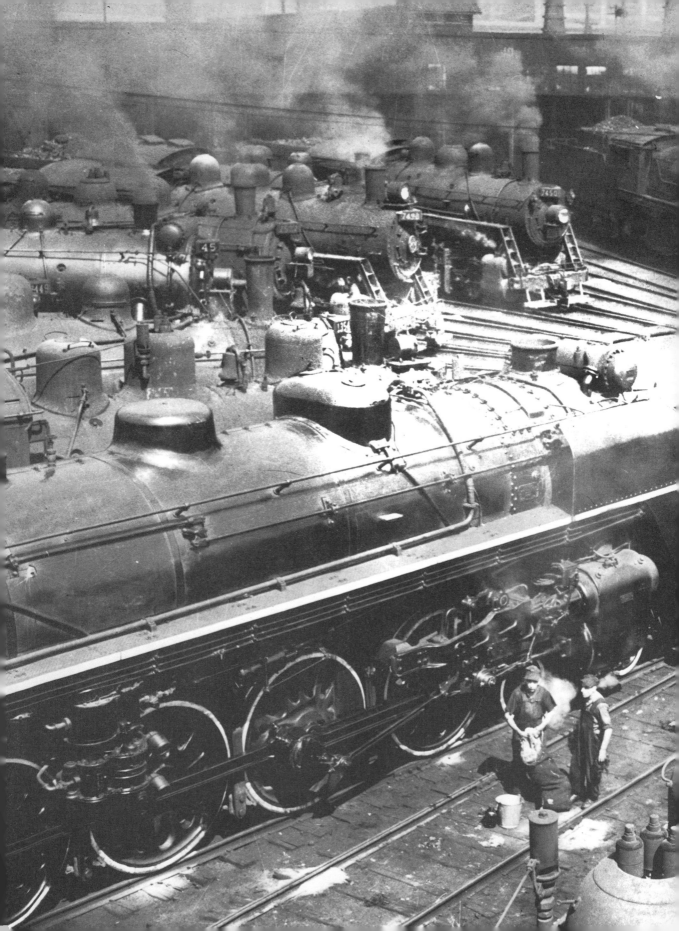

North American trains take the right-hand line on double tracks—the two lines in the foreground are sidings (*E. J. Gulash*)

signals display four distinct aspects only; they are, in fact, very little more difficult to understand than a road traffic light signal. Green means proceed, red means stop, a single yellow means 'proceed at restricted speed expecting to find the next signal at red', while double yellow means 'proceed at medium speed expecting to find the next signal at single yellow'. As we have seen, direction and 'draw-ahead' indications are displayed separately. The whole makes for a very simple and effective system.

In contrast, USA signal aspects are highly complicated; they vary a little from line to line, but taking the Southern Pacific Railroad as an example, seventeen different aspects can be offered, as follows:

ASPECT	MEANING
1. Single Green	Proceed at full speed
2. Single Yellow	Proceed at medium speed
3. Single Red	Stop
4. Double Red	Stop
5. Red over Green	Proceed on diverging route
6. Yellow over Green	Proceed at medium speed. Next signal indicates proceed on diverging route
7. Red over Yellow	Proceed at restricted speed on diverging route
8. Red over Lunar White	Proceed at restricted speed on other than main track
9. Treble Red	Stop

Previous pages:
The dirty job of disposal at the roundhouse (*Canadian National*)

96

10. Double Red over Green	As 5
11. Double Red over Yellow	As 7
12. Double Red over Lunar White	As 8
13. Flashing Red	Proceed at restricted speed, prepared to stop short at any obstruction
14. Flashing Yellow	Proceed prepared to pass next signal at medium speed
15. Double Red and Flashing Yellow	Stop. Then proceed at restricted speed
16. Treble Red and Flashing Yellow	As 15
17. Red and Flashing White	Be governed by timetable

End of the line

The End of the Line is now approaching as *5428* glides along the high iron of the right-hand track of this double track main and, since the fire is being allowed to die down, it's an opportunity to draw a bucketful of warm water and get washed. The hostler—an old term which has survived in America from stage coach days—will take over and see to the quite dirty job of disposal at the roundhouse, once we have come to a stand in the yard reception track.

It has been an interesting night and day for two steam-lovers, although not one of the three locomotives met so far could be regarded as an aristocrat of the steam world. On the other hand, each has been chosen because in its day it was a standard locomotive of medium power for its period and represents the best standard practice of that period: *Actaeon* for the 1840s, *Black Five* for the 1930s and *Forward* for the 1970s. Each was (and in the case of *Forward,* is) exceptionally successful and productive over a wide range of work, more so, I think, than many more glamorous and complex machines such as the *Flying Scotsmans, Chapelons, Niagaras* and *King George Vs*—of the great trains of the recent past.

Some of you may think there has been too little emphasis on handling the controls and too much on knowledge of the railway and its rules and regulations. But that is the way things were and how they remain so today now that diesels and electrics have displaced steam. On the other hand I cannot imagine any disagreement on the emphasis placed on the skill involved in the fireman's task of keeping steam up; and, if handling the controls is usually a fairly simple matter, it must be remembered that the driver as captain of the ship has to take full responsibility for all the fireman does—as well as for all he fails to do—plus all the judgement needed to run the train safely and successfully.

PART TWO:

9

OPPORTUNITIES IN THE REAL WORLD

STEAM PLEASURE LINES AND PRESERVATION

Previous pages:
Steam for pleasure on the continent—similar locomotives run on the Zillertal Railway at Jenbach, Austria, which offers self-drive hire to engine-driving enthusiasts (*Brian Hollingsworth*)

Amateur steam railroading in the USA—the East Broad Top RR, Orbisonia, Pennsylvania (*E. J. Gulash*)

The question implicit in the title of this book can be answered in another way; not 'how does one drive a steam locomotive?' but, instead 'how does one *get* to drive a steam locomotive?' It was pointed out in the introduction that in this day and age, opportunities for the average person to drive or fire a full-size locomotive on a normal working railway are minimal. South Africa for a long time presented an exception by reason of its goverment's racial policies, the ill wind of apartheid. Locomotive crews were in the white sector but whites prepared to take such jobs were in short supply; so, young and enterprising steam enthusiasts from Britain went there specially to serve on the footplate. It is believed that recession and the decline of steam is now discouraging such a ploy and hence budding steam men must fall back on the pleasure railways, or 'daisy-picking' lines, as American jargon calls them.

Steam for pleasure

Fortunately, the steam-for-pleasure railway age has now arrived. It is considered to have started with a narrow gauge line called the Edaville Railroad, built on a cranberry farm at South Carver, Massachusetts in 1947. The first takeover by amateurs of an existing railway was that of the Talyllyn Railway (also narrow gauge) at Towyn, Gwynedd, Wales in 1951.

By 1960 there was sufficient confidence for a group to lease, restore and operate with vintage steam, part of a full-size British Railways branch known as the Bluebell Railway. It runs from Sheffield Park to Horsted Keynes in East Sussex. Since then the movement has gone from strength to strength and, including these three, 308 steam pleasure lines are listed in the author's book *Steam for Pleasure* (Routledge and Kegan Paul, 1978, written with J. B. Snell and P.B. Whitehouse), a world survey. Ninety-three of these are situated in America and 121 in Britain, an indication of the scale of the opportunities which exist.

Package deal instruction

A firm called Travel Britain Company (of Irradion House, Southdown Road, Harpenden, Hertfordshire, UK) goes so far as to offer residential instruction courses in steam locomotive firing and driving on various lines, including the Bluebell Railway, Sussex. Two Austrian local railways offer what they call a *hobbyzug*—a small steam locomotive offered on a self-drive-hire basis. Of course, in this case, instruction is only offered in working the controls and getting the feel of handling the locomotive—there is no pretence of training anyone to take charge on the footplate. The lines in question are the Zillertal Railway at Jenbach near Innsbruck and the Murtal Railway at Murau north of Klagenfurt in Styria (south-east Austria).

But facilities such as this are abnormal and do not apply on the majority of lines. On some of them, in fact, there is little or no scope for the aspiring engine-driver. Nevertheless, on a great many, nothing much more than persistence, coupled with a lack of concern with such a trifling matter as a wage-packet, is necessary to put a person of average intelligence on the footplate of one of the two hundred or so steam-for-pleasure locomotives that puff around on summer days in Britain, America and Europe. It may just happen that railway A has all the footplate help it needs for one particular season; at the same time railway B might well have a situation where a would-be fireman could find himself on the locomotive as a trainee a few minutes after he enquired if they needed anybody. The timing is important; it might well be that on railway B a few weeks later, perhaps after the university vacation had begun, an aspiring volunteer fireman would have got no further than the privilege of cleaning the lavatories. Or railway A might without warning suffer some human crisis and once again need to make newcomers welcome.

Virtually all the pleasure railways have societies which lend support—in many cases they are also the owners. On the whole it is best for volunteers to be members. Some lines will be within reach at

The Talyllyn Railway, Merioneth—the first successful take-over by amateurs (*Brian Hollingsworth*)

weekends, others involve staying away and hence the sacrifice of holiday time; however, in all cases, driving and firing, as they should be, are regarded as jobs to aspire to after a possibly long testing period of willingly, reliably and ably carrying out laborious chores behind the scenes.

The railway on which it is likely to be easiest to succeed is one which is both expanding its services and is remote from industrial Britain. For example, in 1977 the Festiniog Railway in North Wales had to put out a general call to its society members for volunteer firemen; young men who answered the call found themselves, the day

Old GWR 4–4–0 *Earl of Berkeley* on the Bluebell Railway (*J. Ransom*)

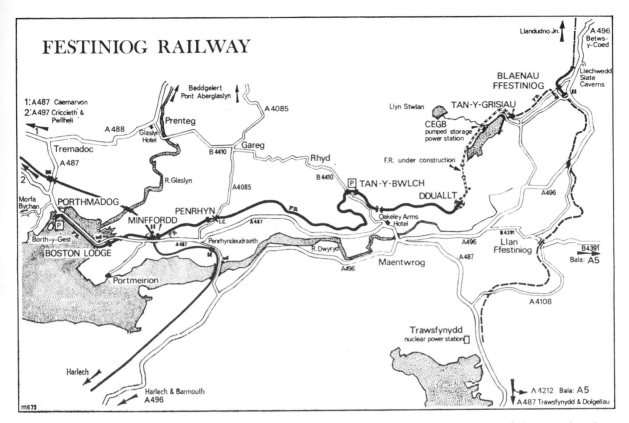

FESTINIOG RAILWAY

26 The route of the Festiniog Railway in North Wales

after arrival at Portmadoc, actually doing the firing and other footplate duties, while the real fireman just kept an eye on what was being done. In 1978 some of these new volunteers will hopefully be passed out to take charge of the fireman's side of the cab by themselves.

Festiniog fireman

During the main summer season the Festiniog Railway has more engines in steam than most—four, in fact, and two of these 'double-manned', ie, in service for so many hours each day that it is considered advisable to change crews around lunchtime. So six drivers and six firemen have to be found, thus increasing the scope for newcomers. One of them, Seamus Rogers (aged 17), describes his experiences below.

"On the day I was to begin work I had been told that I was working the 12.30 train from Porthmadog with [the locomotive] *Linda,* and instructed to arrive at Boston Lodge works at 12 noon (see Fig 26). This I did and, having introduced myself to the driver (Keith Catchpole) and the second man (John Bell), we walked to Boston Lodge Halt where we were to take over the train at the 12.17 crew change.

"As *Linda* rounded the corner below Rhiw Plas bridge and rattled into view my heart leapt—I knew that I was about to realise the ambition of a lifetime. Trying desperately to conceal my excitement

Linda's controls (*Brian Hollingsworth*)

Right:
Festiniog Railway fireman brings the headlamp forward before departure from Porthmadog (*Brian Hollingsworth*)

Linda leaving Porthmadog; the dark smoke indicates a slight excess of oil (*Brian Hollingsworth*)

Right:
Linda a few yards further on—the fireman has now adjusted the oil flow exactly (*Brian Hollingsworth*)

and inexperience from the passengers in the observation car, I climbed aboard and was instructed to sit on the tender—the footplate itself being far too small to accommodate three people.

"The impressions of my first ride across the 'Cob' were ones of extreme regard for comfort and suspension of the carriages—a trip on the footplate of *Blanche,* for example, is an experience that everyone's kidneys should undergo! The change round at Porthmadog seemed swift and efficient and, apart from one difficult moment with a point which I was asked to change (a whim of the Festiniog Railway Signal and Telegraph department is to make life difficult for firemen by ensuring that almost every point lever on the entire system is different from its fellows), I kept pretty much out of the way. I spent the journey up 'observing' the actions of both driver and fireman and periodically being instructed on their duties. I was shown how to change staffs at the end of a token section—normally a station— how to work both the Tan-y-Bwlch and Porthmadog water towers, the

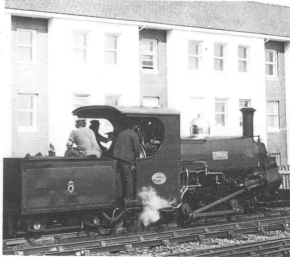

basics of firing and, last but by no means least, how to uncouple and couple the train. This operation, which appears simple when you watch from the platform, ice-cream in hand, while 'the man' does it, is in fact an art known only to those who have suffered embarrassing moments to the delight of the general public, whilst miserably 'making a hash of it'. The simple coupling *is* relatively simple, but it is the pipes for the vacuum brakes which are the devils—apparently possessing minds of their own—and which will, without practice, *never* successfully lock together properly. From all this you will gather that I had some unfortunate moments with them to begin with, but later it cheered me to see other newcomers experiencing similar, or worse, problems—isn't human nature always so? I once saw one poor lad have a total of five attempts at coupling the train at Porthmadog one afternoon, and I did not even wait to see him try to do the vac. pipes! At the end of my first day—two round trips and a putting-the-engine-to-bed session at night, I arrived back at my caravan, met the rest of its inhabitants and retired to bed—my head spinning with everything I had to remember in my new job.

"Over the next few days I was gradually taught the minutiae of the routine and I began firing under the careful scrutiny of the senior man. At the end of the first week I had met many people, been to several parties, and was becoming fairly competent at the job; above all I was enjoying myself.

A fireman's job consists of many more duties than one would suppose for although there are when possible three men on the loco when actually firing, that is, controlling the fire and water in the locomotive, one is constantly at work throughout the entire journey. The third man is responsible for filling the water tanks at Porthmadog and Tan-y-Bwlch, coupling and uncoupling, changing points and watching the train at specific places for the 'OK' signal from the guard.

"The second man, if working an early train, is responsible for checking the burner in the morning and lighting up. Depending on his experience, he will help the driver oil round, or busy himself with cleaning. Once steam is up and the engine has gone over to Porthmadog Harbour, the crew have breakfast, after which the second man will get the water level in the boiler and the pressure at a suitable level for the journey. On departure he has two main functions; firstly, to keep the boiler pressure just below the 'blowing off' mark, and secondly, to keep a good amount of water in the boiler. He remains on the locomotive most of the time as these two relatively simple-sounding jobs are a full time occupation. The basic mechanics of the process are elementary; as the water is put into the boiler via the injector, steam pressure is used up. However, when the injector is not on, the steam pressure, supposing the engine is steaming satisfactorily, gradually builds up. Thus the second man is continually juggling the two levels throughout the trip, trying to keep the pressure high enough to prevent the vacuum brakes being put on automatically, and low enough to prevent the loco blowing off. Similarly with the water level; it must get neither too high, causing the engine to prime, nor too low so that it falls below the crown of the firebox—inviting disaster.

"With oil-firing now universal on the Festiniog, the physical effort of shovelling coal is thankfully a thing remembered by fewer and fewer volunteers, but it must be realised, however, that keeping the fire going is still no easy task. There are two main controls for this: the oil valve from the tender which controls the amount of oil entering the burner, and the atomiser which, by blowing steam in a circular movement around the burner-pan, breaks the oil up into small particles (atomises it), thereby livening the burning and creating a bigger heat. The golden rule I was taught when I first began was: 'Oil up first, atomiser down first'. In this way one ensures that the atomiser does not blow the flames out (which happens quite regularly, especially on windy days), and the oil control and the atomiser are always controlled in a scale in proportion to each other and go 'up' and 'down' at the same moment.

"In fact, it is the constant fear of all new firemen that the fire will blow out on an up journey as this necessitates an un-scheduled stop while it is re-lit. On the down journey with the train 'free-wheeling' one may do it on the move. If one's reactions are lightning quick and supposing that one has even noticed that it has gone out, (this is not as obvious as it might sound), the fire may be re-lit by a swift increase on the oil control in the hope that it will light itself from the still glowing firebox surrounds. If not, however, the oil is turned down, a piece of rag soaked with 'de-greaser' pushed into the end of the inspection hole on the fire hole door, lit, and pushed onto the burner. The oil and atomiser should then be turned up again and the fire should be alight.

"At the Boston Lodge end of the 'Cob' on the up journey, both oil and atomiser are wound up as the driver opens the regulator for the climb. The idea is very simple; as the driver opens the regulator the oil goes up, as he shuts it, the oil goes down. Likewise when he moves from pilot valve into main valve, and vice versa. When approaching stations the oil must be turned down fractionally before the driver shuts the regulator to rule out the frightening effect of entering the platform with a towering column of thick black oily smoke emerging in a horrifying cloud from the chimney—this is not popular with the local inhabitants, many of whom have nearby washing lines! The only problem arises here when, as one enters the station, the pressure comes up with the close of the regulator. In this instance, to prevent blowing off, one must put on the injector *and* turn down the oil almost instantaneously with only one pair of hands. This is an experience which my adrenalin enjoyed rather too frequently for my liking.

"Shortly after leaving Minffordd, when the loco is opened right out for the ascent of the formidable Gwyndy bank, a scoop of sand is thrown into the firebox. The strong blast pulls the sand through the tubes, scouring away the sooty deposits which had formed inside them. A spectacular black cloud bursts out of the chimney, tactfully arranged so that it occurs at the exact moment when the loco is passing the Penrhyndeudraeth town rubbish dump.

"The third man's job is far more relaxing. Whilst on the move he may sit back on the tender and enjoy the trip, only periodically needing to check with the guard that all is well with the train. At Porthmadog and Tan-y-bwlch he must fill the water tank, a job which generally presents few problems except occasionally at Porthmadog where people sometimes manage to jam the cock so tightly shut that one is obliged to swing bodily on the chain to move it—a humiliating exhibition when you are watched by intrigued and amused members of the public from the platform. Other than this the third man changes points, including the lever frame at Porthmadog and, as already mentioned, couples up. In addition to these duties, however, he has the delightful task of staff 'changes'; if stations are manned these changes are done by the station master and the staff is passed to the loco crew, usually whilst the train is on the move. The latter manoeuvre is yet another exciting moment as the possibility is that if a staff is dropped it will either bend and then not go back into the instrument properly, or else it will go through the window of the observation car—a thing feared, but luckily so far avoided.

When stations are unmanned the third man, armed with the engine's keys, leaps off upon entering the station, proceeds to the instrument house, unlocks it, enters and inserts the staff into the appropriate instrument. He next rings 'Control', from whom he requests permission to draw the next section's token: permission granted, he winds the generator to obtain release, and removes the new staff. He then re-locks the shed and proceeds down the platform to the loco, trying to avoid the gaze of ranks of small boys (and parents!) all of whom find something interesting in every action he commits.

"That is, in brief, an outline of the basic job. However, every trip is different and each loco behaves differently every day. The weather, too, can cause some excitement; rain, which fell frequently throughout my stay, poses traction problems, and starting away from any of the intermediate stations on a wet day is quite nerve-racking. As the train gets under way, the oil control is wound up and suddenly the engine loses her feet and, with a frantic spinning, tries to regain them, once again shooting the dreaded column of black smoke into the equally black sky. With this likely to happen, one's reactions have to be lightning quick.

"Once we had three emergency stops on one journey. After leaving Porthmadog with a mid-day train, the first emergency occurred half way over the 'Cob', just as I was settling down into the routine. Suddenly the regulator was slammed shut, the brakes were swiftly applied and, before I could stop it, a fearsome column of black haze rose from the chimney. It appeared that a care-free family crossing the 'Cob' had not seen the train and were just manoeuvring their pram onto the track! Hearing a sharp blast on the whistle they turned to see the train screeching to a halt almost upon them. I don't think I have ever seen a pram move quite so quickly—it was whisked out of the way in a flash and, after a polite word of warning from the driver, we continued on our way. The second sudden stop happened between

Minffordd and Penrhyn, just off Gwyndy Bank—once again, more smoke! This time it was a mechanical fault, and the driver had felt the engine suddenly 'tighten'; there was, I gathered, a warm bearing. We proceeded gently to the terminus with periodic oilings and by Rhiw Goch on the down trip, it had cooled down thanks to some adjustment made at Llyn Ystradau. The passengers had already had two lots of unexpected excitement for their money when, after crossing the road at Penrhyn, we perceived a dog on the track on the approach to the station. Not wanting to risk hitting it, we once more were forced to make an unscheduled stop, more gently this time, as we were travelling at a slower speed. It is hard to imagine what impression that particular trainload of passengers had of the railway!

"I much enjoyed my time as a trainee engineman and intend to return to work again next summer. I think it is a credit to those who work on the Festiniog Railway, both permanently and as volunteers, that they manage to create such a welcoming atmosphere and an excellent social life."

It should perhaps be added that a fully trained Festiniog fireman combines the duties of the partially trained second and third man mentioned in this account. Normally there are only two men on Festiniog footplates. One might also comment that the type of oil burner used on the FR, in which the flame is swirled round about a vertical axis, is more sensitive to variations in the supply of atomising steam, than the more normal type (as fitted to the dream locomotive *Forward*) in which the flame swirls around a transverse one.

Standard gauge and coal firing
Volunteer drivers and firemen have a much harder time on a coal-burning railway, particularly if it is standard gauge and uses large locomotives. Professional old-time steam enginemen, although they might have worked harder on the run, at least would not have to raise steam and put the engine to bed (to use the nursery phrase) after each day's operations. Raising steam on *5428* for a nine o'clock start meant an all-night session at the shed. A little unprofessionally we used several firelighters—several packets in fact—to light up. Building up the fire and in time bringing 1,200 gallons of water in the boiler to the boil is a very slow business; five hours is normal, from all cold. Cleaning is also a point; pleasure railways have no option but to display their locomotives in band-box condition, whatever was the custom on big brother in the later years of steam.

So the crew starts the day's running several hours to the bad; then after the work is over the fire has to be dropped and the ashpan and smokebox emptied. Bright parts must be oiled or greased to prevent corrosion, having regard to the period of idleness which so often, on a typical present-day steam line, must elapse before the next outing.

As regards the number of volunteer enginemen required, a rather different situation appertains on many of the standard gauge lines as well as the less busy narrow gauge ones, where to have more than one

Amateur drivers are not welcome on the Silverton Train run along the Canyon of the Lost Souls! (*Brian Hollingsworth*)

engine in steam is exceptional. Coupled with this are the facts that a lot of these lines are handy for weekend volunteers and the services they run outside the weekends are minimal. Accordingly, the scope for newcomers is sometimes limited. Even so, steam for pleasure is expanding and new little 'puff up and down on Sunday' operations are constantly coming into being. Soon enough the novelty wears off and the less dedicated spirits melt away; while someone persistent, willing to slog away weekend after weekend, might quite quickly find himself training and doubling as fireman or driver.

The impossibles are those where footplate crews are provided by 'big brother' and problems of union membership and seniority arise. British Railway's Vale of Rheidol line, the Denver to Rio Grande Western Railroad's Silverton train and, until recently Puffing Billy near Melbourne, Australia, are famous operations that come under this heading. In the same category comes the operation of steam locomotives on such main-line systems as British Rail, Canadian National, Union Pacific and Southern Railway (of USA). Even here difficulties sometimes arise because the crew to whom a particular steam duty is allocated by rotation may in fact be a little rusty or inexperienced in steam traction. On the other hand, it is often the case in Britain that some volunteers for footplate duties on many pleasure lines are in fact professional locomotive crews keeping their hand in on steam. Such people provide a vital and fortunately infectious element of professionalism amongst the amateurs.

It has been suggested that the quickest way on to a footplate is as a

Only professional BR footplate staff drive on the Vale of Rheidol line at Aberystwyth, Wales (*Brian Hollingsworth*)

A preliminary to engine-driving (*J. Ransom*)

volunteer willing to work long hours (often mid-week) without pay. Not everybody is able to do this—very few indeed for an extended period—and the larger and busier pleasure railways do also employ both full-time and seasonal paid staff. With the dubious proposition that one cannot expect munificent pay for enjoying a favourite sport, it must be said that the rates of pay are low; but for this reason such jobs are occasionally not too hard to come by, particularly for anyone who has already some relevant experience.

Steam survival

So, in these late 1970s, steam driving men look to their survival as providers of pleasure. One cloud only has appeared above the horizon, as yet 'no bigger than a man's hand' and this is the problem of major renewals. It is less of a problem on the narrow gauge—witness the renewed 'double Fairlie' 0–4–4–0 *Earl of Merioneth* on the Festiniog Railway. But in standard gauge the cost of a major overhaul is so high as to be prohibitive.

So far the operators have relied on a process akin to Lewis Carroll's Alice-in-Wonderland Mad Hatter's tea party. Having put together a collection of discarded BR and other steam locomotives, each with a residue of usable mileage before overhaul, they bring them into service in succession; later they are discarded when this mileage has been used up. One might cite the example of the Keighley & Worth Valley Railway—one of the best firms in the business—who have

Lady Joan of the Knebworth Park and Wintergreen Railway (*Pleasurerail Limited*)

thirty-five steam locomotives on the property, of which eleven might be regarded as discarded. Recently as few as two were available for use.

Incidentally, on most lines tight bridges and clearances preclude the running in Britain of locomotives from countries abroad, where supplies are still available. An exception is the Nene Valley Railway near Peterborough, England, where volunteer engine crews get experience of German, French and Swedish steam. Even so, the time is coming when the standard-gauge lines will have to fund major overhauls and this places a big question mark over the future.

New 'puff up and down on Sunday' operations are constantly coming into being (*Brian Hollingsworth*)

10

OPPORTUNITIES IN A MINIATURE WORLD

STEAM RAILWAYS FROM 15 in. GAUGE DOWN TO 7¼ in.

Even should the worst come to the worst and the operation of full-size steam become totally impossible economically, the would-be engine driver can take heart from there being another way. The immense cost of making and repairing parts of full-size steam locomotives is mainly due to their great weight and size. A connecting rod, for example, weighs perhaps 500 lb, and this considerable weight is reflected both in the cost of the original steel forging from which it is made and the amount of machining needed to shape it into the finished product.

Should you decide to make a replica to, say, one-fifth of the full size, the weight of this connecting rod goes down, not by five times but by five × five × five, that is, 125 times. Therefore the model connecting rod will weigh a mere 4 lb. This applies to all components, even—in approximate terms—to the fuel consumed, and it brings the expense of making and repairing them down into quite another category. One feels that on grounds of cost the time is coming when opportunities to drive steam will be more common on miniature railways than on full-size ones.

Miniature pioneer

The father of the miniature railway was a man by the name of Sir Arthur Percival Heywood of Duffield Bank, near Derby, who in 1865

Sir Arthur Percival Heywood's railway at Duffield Bank: 0–6–0T *Ella* and freight train at Tennis Ground station (*Author's collection*)

Heywood designed and built 15 in. gauge steam locomotives with his own hands, some named after his own daughters (*Author's collection*)

Right:
Ready for action on 'the greatest little railway in the world'—the Romney, Hythe & Dymchurch Railway (*T. Crowhurst*)

began construction of a 15 in. gauge line on his far from level estate. He designed and built, largely with his own hands, a succession of little steam locomotives—named after his daughters—of original design and concept.

Heywood's locomotives were miniatures but they were not models in the sense of being recognizable miniature replicas of full-size locomotives. The pioneering of these was left to Heywood's successors, that is to the partnership of Wenman Bassett-Lowke as the businessman and Henry Greenly as the designer and engineer. Their 15 in. gauge *Little Giant* 4–4–2 took the rails at Blackpool in 1910.

It has become the custom that, whilst any replica less than full-size can be spoken of correctly as either model, little or miniature, the arbitrary distinction generally used in the railway enthusiast world is that model locomotives are too small to ride on and miniature ones are sufficiently large to be ridden on by their drivers. In practice, miniature railways are those with gauges between $7\frac{1}{4}$ in. and 20 in.

Romney, Hythe & Dymchurch

The greatest of the miniatures—at one time it called itself 'the biggest little railway in the world'—is the famous Romney, Hythe & Dymchurch Railway, now over fifty years old, which runs thirteen miles along the south coast of Britain from Hythe near Folkestone to Dungeness. The RH & DR has a fleet of ten steam locomotives of one-third full size. One is oil-burning, the remainder coal. Five are replicas of 4–6–2 locomotives from the old LNER, two are similar but built as 4–8–2s. There are two 4–6–2s of North American inspiration and one of German, giving an even more international flavour to the line than the railway in our dream. In order to man these locomotives during the short period in the summer when the peak tourist service is being run, temporary drivers are engaged and for anyone for whom the low rates of pay are acceptable, vacancies do sometimes arise.

One very distinctive point about all miniature steam locomotives is that the driver has to do the fireman's job as well; on the RH&DR two

A comparison between the *Flying Scotsman* 4–6–2 in full size and Romney, Hythe & Dymchurch *Southern Maid* 4–6–2 to one third scale (*G. A. Barlow*)

people can be accommodated (with a squeeze) in the cab while a driver is training, but after that he is on his own with the full responsibility of both jobs. Of course, instead of firing 35 lb of coal each minute, one fires five, and this gives the driver-fireman time to see to everything else.

Fortunately, fifty years ago the great Henry Greenly did a fabulous job when he designed the original locomotives. Their reliability and ease of working is one factor that makes one-man operation possible, although the tradition of good enginemanship at New Romney is another. The length of the railway is thirteen miles and, since one terminal station is arranged in a great circular loop, for special occasions a twenty-six-mile non-stop run is possible. Because the line is a miniature to one-third full-size, this is the equivalent of seventy-eight miles—a very respectable run, taking $1\frac{1}{4}$ hours to perform. The equivalent speed is seventy-five miles per hour, so driving on the RH&DR is real main-line operation, not the branch or local running which is all that is possible in full size, outside unionised BR. In fact, the way one drives and fires the Romney coal-burners as well as the oil-burner differs virtually not at all from how we drove and fired the

Canadian style 4–6–2
Winston Churchill ready to
leave Hythe on the Romney,
Hythe & Dymchurch
Railway (*Romney, Hythe &
Dymchurch Railway*)

Controls of a 7¼ in. 4–4–0
Colossus, built by R. Marsh,
owned by R. Jones (*W.
Jones*)

Right:
'A tank full' at Hythe
(*A. R. W. Crowhurst*)

locomotives of our dream. In Hitchcock's film masterpiece *The Lady Vanishes*, Michael Redgrave has no problems in driving Margaret Lockwood and the Orient Express out of trouble because, as he explains, 'I once drove an engine on the Dymchurch line.' Although the RH&DR has some financial problems because of its length, much of which is double track, these are not associated with the cost of keeping its steam fleet in operation over fifty years.

Smaller still

Smaller-sized public miniature railways exist but, as size decreases so does similarity to full-size. This is not so much in the technique of driving but in the position. On 15 in. gauge there is no room in the cab—the driver has to sit in the tender—but at least his head is below

Forest Railway Rio Grande 2–8–2 *General Palmer* approaches the main station at full speed with owner driving (*Forest Railway*)

Model of Union Pacific *Big Boy* under construction for the Forest Railway (*Severn-Lamb Limited*)

the cab roof and he looks out through the front spectacle or over the side as per big sister. In $10\frac{1}{4}$ in. gauge, which is the next 'standard' size down, you sit in or on the tender but, unless some very odd prototype is chosen, the driver's head and shoulders are well outside the cab. Similar remarks apply to $7\frac{1}{4}$ in. gauge.

There are many such lines in what journalistically might be called a growth industry—75% or more, alas, are diesel or petrol 'kiddies' rides'. The remainder cover the whole spectrum from being completely public and commercial—and often the owner's means of livelihood—to being completely private, that is, by invitation only. In the middle are those which run regularly but, say, on summer Sundays only and the public are invited in to help defray some of the expenses.

Forest Railway
A commercial example is the $7\frac{1}{4}$ in. gauge Forest Railway in the

village of Dobwalls, near Liskeard, Cornwall. It operates daily in the summer and curves in and out of the trees of a substantial plantation. There are complex spirals, deep cuttings, fly-overs, embankments and long tunnels, which carry names like Lost Souls Canyon, Sherman Summit, Toltec Tunnel and Windy Point. From this you may guess that the ambience is that of the Western USA and this is reflected in the locomotive fleet which includes a wonderful working replica of the famous Union Pacific *Big Boy* 4–8–8–4. Driving on such a line is a great thrill, but as we found on the full-size Cornish railway, continuously changing curves and gradients—up to 1 in 25 or 4%— mean unwinking concentration.

Hilton Valley Railway

A Sundays-and-holidays only example is the Hilton Valley Railway at Hilton, near Bridgnorth in Shropshire, which runs a service in real 'jazz' style with steam trains every few minutes. Crossing at loops along the $7\frac{1}{4}$ in. gauge single line is precisely controlled by a very neat and correct signalling system. Operation is entirely in the hands of unpaid volunteers and, as usual, willingness to help plus reliability are the passports to acceptance here.

The public is admitted on Sunday afternoons and a couple of hours or so before opening time the depôt is humming with steam-raising activity. The shed roads are set at waist level in order to make preparation and maintenance easier, on locomotives which measure a mere 2 ft. or less from the rail to the tip of the chimney. On this size it takes from half- to three-quarters of an hour from putting a match to the kindling in the firebox to having steam. Artificial draught is provided by a blower system, as these little chimneys have no natural draught of their own. While the water is heating, there is time to fill

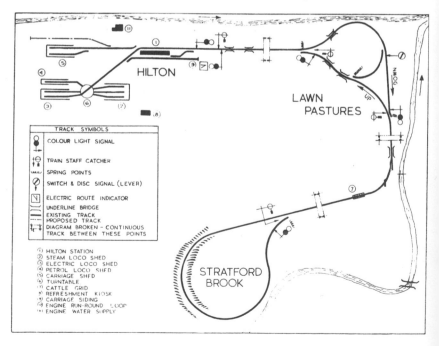

27 Diagram of the Hilton Valley Railway (not to scale)

118

Hilton Valley Railway—the author's Garratt type loco *Mount Kilimanjaro* hauls 117 people on the occasion of the line's 21st Birthday (*J. Adams*)

Hilton Valley Railway—handing over the staff (*Hilton Valley Railway*)

Hilton Queen and *Lorna Doone*—on the 7¼ in. gauge Hilton Valley Railway (*R. Moore*)

Right:
David Curwen, well-known constructor of miniature locomotives, drives his 0–4–2T *Fanny* 'hands off' (*Brian Hollingsworth*)

A miniature steam locomotive factory—Milner Engineering Limited of Chester (*Milner Engineering*)

the lubricator, oil round, as well as give a general clean and polish, always easier when things have got warm.

At Hilton the spectacle is provided by lots of action and, as in full size, the problem is keeping steam up and running the train, rather than just driving. A train every four minutes is the rule and precision working is necessary to keep traffic moving without a hitch, with three or four trains in action simultaneously on the little railroad. If you are wholly responsible for one of them, there is absolutely no time for day-dreaming. Incidentally, the Hilton goes one further than the Romney in that you are not only driver and fireman, but wearing the guard's hat as well. However, a 100% bonus on the standard rate of pay is offered for these extra duties!

Well, there one is at the head of a train in Hilton station with the customers piling on—about thirty of them—weighing with the train all of two tons. A train rolls in on the other line, the electric points are thrown, the colour-light starting signal changes to green and so 'right-away'. This is a ridiculous load for a small engine and it means jockeying with the regulator to get away, at the same time not forgetting to pick up the tablet (drinks all round in the *Black Lion* afterwards, if one forgets) for the section to Lawn Pastures (see Fig 27). Time now to pop a bit on the fire while the blast is strong as she accelerates to a nice running speed along this fairly straight and level length. Ease up for the spring-worked points and the sharp curves of the passing loop, hang the tablet on the catcher provided, glance back as the train sweeps round the loop line in the trees, to see that all is well with the train. If all is to time a train will be heard running by on the other side of the loop, timed just right to cross us without stopping.

Amongst occasions when a meet at Lawn Pastures did not go according to plan must be mentioned an occasion when the fire of the author's oil-burning loco *Mount Kilimanjaro* went out and he, having left behind the matches, was reduced to trying to borrow from the passengers . . . none of them had any!

Nineteen times out of twenty the starting signal will be showing green and the token in its place at the other end of the loop, as the locomotive is opened out for the climb to Stratford Brook. Here there is a reversing loop and yet another tablet catcher—with another train waiting for us to run in. That in its turn picks up the tablet and proceeds while we have a welcome breather with an opportunity to top up the tank and set the fire to rights, before the next spell of non-stop action. Both locomotive and driver need this; particularly when you think that some of the Hilton locomotives are scale models of one-eighth full size and to them a thirty-passenger load is the equivalent of a 1,000 ton train.

Almost before we know it there comes the sound of another hard-pressed locomotive approaching and it is time to be going. The return trip is a mirror image of the outward one except that the 'rest' period at the end terminus is entirely taken up with turning the locomotive on the turntable, servicing it and running round to the front end of the train. So the long afternoon wears on, reflecting exactly what full-size locomotive drivers know, that the hardest and trickiest (also the least well-paid) turn is the humble all-stations local rather than the glamorous long-distance express.

Private miniature railways

Private miniature railways are essentially more modest; the writer's opportunities for running steam locomotives are now confined to one with which he is very fully involved. Its design and concept is best set down in the terms of the official guide-book . . .

CROESOR JUNCTION & PACIFIC
Miniature rails in miniature mountains

"The Croesor Junction and Pacific Railway is a private garden line built to $7\frac{1}{4}$ in. gauge. It is of narrow gauge style; the choice of scale was dictated by the width of that part of the human form used for sitting down, it being desired to sit IN rather than ON the locomotives when driving.

"The name? Well, the famous Croesor Junction between the Welsh Highland Railway and the Croesor Tramway had its brief life within 100 yards or so of the house gate. Furthermore, if you go far enough in any direction you will eventually reach the Pacific, but lines with Pacific in their names traditionally never reach there!

"The first sod was turned (with due ceremony) in September 1974 and three years later, work reached a point where a push-and-pull train could be operated under construction conditions, over a 180 yards length.

"The house at Creua is situated 60 ft above the gate, where there is a suitable site for a station, but only 800 ft away horizontally. Therefore to reduce the ruling gradient to an acceptable 4.5% (1 in 22), the traditional ruses of mountain railway engineering will have to be adopted, viz, one zig-zag reverse and spiral. In the summer of 1977 the line laid took the simplest form for gaining height in the mountains, a U-turn across the valley, round the house, involving a 50 ft long bridge, with three 10 ft and one 20 ft spans, across the Afon Creua. The present total height gain of the line is around 20 ft.

From David Curwen of Devizes came Rio Grande 2–8–2 *Queen of Colorado* (*Brian Hollingsworth*)

Incidentally, 4.5% is the ruling gradient of the Rio Grande line.

"On the 'main line' the curvature is generally better than 50 ft radius, but a spur leading to the locomotive depot is at the minimum allowable radius of 35 ft. The depot—which is of roundhouse form—is served by a 19 ft 6 in. turntable. All the track is laid from 14 lb/yd BS Mines steel rail, fixed by coach screws and washers to jarrah sleepers, each 4 × 2 × 22 in. and spaced at 2 ft centres. Wheel treads, etc. follow $10\frac{1}{4}$ in. rather than $7\frac{1}{4}$ in. standards.

"The present locomotive fleet represents spectacular mountain railroading in far away places, to wit, America, Asia and Africa.

"From David Curwen of Devizes in 1968, came a model of one of the famous Denver and Rio Grande Western class K-36 2–8–2s used on that company's narrow gauge lines in the Rockies. This is No. 487 *Queen of Colorado*.

"Then, in 1973, Coleby-Simkins of Stapleford delivered No. 784 *Kanchenjunga*, a Darjeeling-Himalayan saddle and well tank. In 1975 from the same builders came East African Railways No. 5928 *Mount Kilimanjaro,* representing the longest and most powerful steam locomotive running in the world today. Finally, in October 1977,

Mountain railways are dominated by the problems of traction going up and braking coming down (*Brian Hollingsworth*)

122

Darjeeling-Himalayan
on the Croesor Junction &
Pacific Railway 0–4–0T
Kanchenjunga (*Brian
Hollingsworth*)

Right:
Wood-burning 2–8–0
Shoshone on the Croesor
Junction & Pacific Railway
(*A. R. W. Crowhurst*)

Milner Engineering of Chester supplied diamond-stacker Rio Grande 2–8–0 No. 402 *Shoshone*.

"None of the models are super-detailed but are intended to give a working illusion of their big sisters at a fraction of the running costs. These are reduced approximately in proportion to the cube of the scale, that is 125 to 1 in the case of the two Rio's.

"The rolling stock is currently not notable. That for passengers consisting of ride-astride type (self-braking and stabilising, because people instinctively put their feet on the ground if problems arise), plus a few dubious freight vehicles loosely based on Rio Grande prototypes, at present used and abused for construction purposes. Couplings are link and pin type.

"It is intended that the CJ&PR will operate under a simplified version of the incredible American Standard Operating Rules, ie, basically by timetable and superiority of direction but modifiable with all the fascinating complexities of extras, second sections and train orders handed up on forked sticks. Nevertheless, the CJ&PR will remain a railway and not a railroad."

Driving on the Croesor & Pacific is dominated (as are all mountain railroads with gradients steeper than 1 in 40 or 2.5%) by the problems of maintaining traction going uphill and braking coming down. A friend of the writer's remarked, when the railway was in contemplation, that the CJ&P would be the only one in the world where drivers would be issued with parachutes. It has not turned out as badly as that, but certainly the gradients stretch the skill of the drivers and the capability of the locomotives to the utmost.

Also, having solved the problems with one locomotive, say *Queen of Colorado* with its wide firebox, one can try using *Shoshone* which has a narrow one or *Kilimanjaro* which is an oil-burner. It is fascinating to find how closely the comparative performance of the replicas relate to full-size. Indeed, this is one of the greatest charms as well as being possibly the *raison d'être* of all these hundreds of miniature steam lines in Britain, the USA and elsewhere.

11

BUILD AND RUN YOUR OWN

THE LIVE STEAM CLUBS

We have seen that, while the driving of steam locomotives is a most stimulating and challenging thing to do, it is also so fraught that those who own or control them are reluctant to allow their use by anyone who is in any way an unknown quantity. Hence the rather discouraging and ambiguous tone of previous chapters.

There is one way out of this *impasse* and that is to be the person who owns the locomotive. It may surprise you to learn that over one hundred cities and towns in Britain have clubs complete with tracks on which members can drive their own locomotives. In America the movement is equally large and in other English-speaking countries proportionately quite big.

The first thing that must be said in explanation is that size is critical. Private people have owned and driven their own full-size locomotives—the writer is one of them—but those incredible days of ten years ago, when British Railways were selling off steam express locomotives in ready-to-roll condition for the price of a moderate family car, have now disappeared for ever. On the whole and except for millionaires, the attainment of private ownership of a full-size steam locomotive is now a thing of the past.

Fundamental simplicity

There is, however, an alternative and it is this—because of its fundamental simplicity, the steam locomotive lends itself to reproduction in miniature without any change in the basic principles of its operation. For example, a model locomotive can be built one-sixteenth full-size—what in model engineering is called $\frac{3}{4}$ in. to 1 ft scale—and obtain adequate power from a coal fire burning in a grate as little as 6 in. long by 2 in. wide. It will also haul the person who drives it. An illustration of the way in which the problems reduce is the fact that in theory the weight (and to some extent the cost) of the whole locomotive as well as its individual parts comes down not sixteen times but sixteen × sixteen × sixteen = 4,096 times; a typical 70 ton BR 4–6–0 locomotive becomes a model of 38 lb. In practice, construction of a reasonably robust working model is a little more massive than one exactly to scale in all details so, for example, the

George Barlow, running superintendent of the Romney Hythe & Dymchurch Railway, takes a busman's holiday (*W. Jones*)

Archeological relics? No, a set of castings for a live steam locomotive (*Milner Engineering*)

GWR 4–6–0 shown weighs 55 lb, still an easy one-man lift.

The beauty of such a model is that all the instruction given in the earlier chapters of this book applies in the small size almost without modification; the principal difference, of course, is that with a driver 18 in. wide and a cab $7\frac{1}{2}$ in. wide there can be no separation between the fireman's and the driver's side—one person has to do both jobs. In fact, the driver does not sit on or in such a locomotive; instead, he usually rides astride a flat car coupled on behind; the track being raised above the ground. But all the essential handles are there just the same and need to be worked in just the same way to produce just the same noises, effects and results.

Magazines

In order to get to drive a steam locomotive via this route a reasonable start would be to take in either the British fortnightly magazine *Model Engineer* (PO Box 35, Hemel Hempstead, Herts, England HP1 1EE) or the American monthly *Live Steam* (PO Box 286, Cedillac, Michigan, 49601 USA). One might then proceed by joining the local club (a list is given in the Appendix on p 145), perhaps first paying a visit to see what goes on at the track.

Among the features of both *Model Engineer* and *Live Steam* magazines are detailed serial articles on how to build steam locomotives oneself. This is certainly the cheapest way of getting to drive one's own steam locomotive but whilst every facility in the way of castings, parts and tools are readily available, it would be facile to suggest that even the simplest passenger-hauling locomotive would take less than two years of spare time to construct.

Tools for the job

A metal-turning lathe, power drill, plus the usual hand tools, files, taps and dies, work bench, vice, welding and brazing equipment, form the minimum requirement for undertaking such a task. All this equipment is readily available, and, of course, a spin-off worth having at the end of the two years would be a valuable knowledge of its use. Moreover, the actual construction of a steam locomotive will teach a person how they work better than columns of writing.

It is certainly possible to buy completed locomotives, either second-hand or commissioned specially from a reputable builder. In either case one definite rule applies — do not part with money until you have tried her in steam. Buying second-hand can be as dubious as horse trading; a good way is to buy direct from a fellow member of a live steam club. Then one is, first, likely to have ample evidence on performance; second, advice on whether the price asked is a fair one is likely to be available; third, the substantial mark-up of a dealer has not got to be paid. As regards commissioning a locomotive to be built specially, the snag is that 1,000 plus man-hours of skilled work have to be paid for and one need not be an economist or estimator to realise the kind of sum that involves at present-day rates.

Construction

The actual task of construction is as far removed as one could imagine from the normal plastic model kit. Each part has to be shaped from metal to precise dimensions; holes have to be bored dead square, round parts turned dead true and so on. As received from the suppliers, the set of castings and special materials appears to be a collection of crude and shapeless random bits of metal. For a smallish $3\frac{1}{2}$ in. gauge locomotive suitable for a beginner, a set would (at 1977 prices) cost around £60. Perhaps another £30 would go in metal sheet, rod and bar material, nuts and bolts etc, to complete the engine chassis and the tender. It may be that a first-timer should, if he possibly could, order a completed boiler (£120). As an extravagance, to get the locomotive more quickly on to the road, a complete set of steam fittings would set him back a further £45 or so over and above the cost of materials to make them.

What to build

Sets of castings for perhaps one hundred different locomotives — from 0-4-0 to 2-10-0 — are available in England and similarly in North America. Drawings are available for all and books of instruction for a few — the latter are the ones that the beginner would be wise to favour.

The majority of the designs and the books available are the work of

The author drives an 'LBSC' Black Five on the track of the Brighouse and Halifax Society of Model Engineers (*C. Hollingsworth*)

28 *Virginia* designed by
'LBSC'

A 5 in. gauge LMS Jubilee
4–6–0 on the track at Kinver
near Stourbridge (*Brian
Hollingsworth*)

Jackie Jones drives *Mabel*,
built by 'LBSC' (*R. Jones*)

one man, who for forty years or so worked sixteen hours a day both to perfect the small steam locomotive and to instruct in its construction and operation. 'Curly' Lawrence—under the pseudonym 'LBSC'— wrote for the tyro, the man for whom a vice was something to be ashamed of and a tap was just for drawing water. Alas, in 1967 he moved on to that 'Last Great Engine Shed in the Sky' but the 2,500 or so articles (many collected in book form) that he wrote and the eighty locomotive designs that he produced, remain as his legacy for our advantage (see Fig 28).

The costs specified above are based on one of these designs, a 'Wild West' American style 4–4–0 which he called *Virginia*—the sort of locomotive that, when trouble comes, expects Gary Cooper to ride up and set things right. The construction of *Virginia* was described in the *Model Engineer* during 1956–7, but the articles are available in book form, at the time of writing.

A beginner could graduate to a locomotive like Lawrence's $3\frac{1}{2}$ in. gauge Black Five—he called her *Doris*—described in 1948–9. In this case no book is available, but this is no detriment, because *Doris* is no first-attempt locomotive. Experience gained in constructing one loco 'by the book' would enable a second to be made from drawings, which are readily available.

A small edition of this book's locomotive *Forward* would represent a further stage of self-development for the budding live steam man—a doctor's degree, if you like. In this case he would have to do much of the design himself, helped by similar designs from the work of Lawrence and his successors. It would be necessary for him to make up his own patterns from which special castings could be produced, although, since much of *Forward* is standard North American, some parts available there might be used.

No kits of parts

One would like to be able to say that a middle course was possible in the form of a kit of parts, whereby the really difficult machining could be done on a factory production line, whilst the assembly and fitting is left to the builder. The famous house of Stuart Turner, Henley-on-Thames, England, offers such services for model stationary steam engines, but no one so far does it for locomotives. As we have seen standard fittings such as injectors, pumps, valves, gauges, whistles etc, are available and these are of course a help in speeding the great day when a do-it-yourself locomotive turns its wheels under steam for the first time.

The smallest size that will pull the driver is $\frac{1}{2}$ in. to 1 ft scale, that is $2\frac{1}{2}$ in. gauge. But a human load stretches this size to the limit and hence drive-yourself locomotives are best built one size up, in $\frac{3}{4}$ in. scale or $3\frac{1}{2}$ in. gauge. If it is a case of drive-your-friends as well, then 5 in. ($4\frac{3}{4}$ in. in America) is the size, and many live steam clubs make their expenses by offering rides with locomotives in this size. A typical club raised track offers both 5 in. and $3\frac{1}{2}$ in. (sometimes $2\frac{1}{2}$ in. as well) on three or four rails.

Railway wrecks in $3\frac{1}{2}$ in. gauge are not the serious matter they are in full size (*Author's collection*)

A run with a little locomotive

What is it like to take such a locomotive for a run on one of these railways? First, the locomotive has (according to the attitude of the domestic authorities) either to be taken down from its pedestal or extracted from its hiding place, cleaned, checked and carried out to the car. Next, all the paraphernalia of a miniature running shed, fire-irons, coal, kindling, two kinds of oil, tool box, steam raising blower and a few spare parts have to be collected; then, away to the site of the track.

Most club lines have steam raising sidings, connected to the main line by a traverser or turntable, since ordinary points and turnouts

A $3\frac{1}{2}$ in. gauge locomotive cab; from left to right the controls are: water gauge blowdown, regulator, blower, injector steam, reversing screw and below right, water-pump by-pass (*Brian Hollingsworth*)

are not practicable on a raised track. It is on one of these sidings that operations begin. The natural draught which can be relied on to keep the fire alight and raise steam on big sister is inadequate for the little one, so a forced draught is needed, provided usually by an electrically driven blower adapted to suck from the chimney.

After the crucial check to see if there is water in the boiler—just the same, you see—we set up the blower, and switch on. The fire is started with some rag soaked in paraffin, then pieces of wood or charcoal are fed in through the firehole door. When properly alight, the fire can be built up with coal broken up into pieces which vary in size from a pea—the minimum—to a gooseberry.

In ten minutes or so the needle of the steam gauge leaves the pin and slowly begins to build up. Compare this with the time for steam-raising in full size, which involves several hours waiting. In miniature one has barely time to get around the bearings with an oil-can, top up the cylinder lubricator tank and fill the tender with water, operations which differ hardly at all in time between the two sizes.

When pressure has built up to, say, 20 lb per sq. in. the locomotive's own blower can be turned on and the external blower dispensed with. Then and there she comes alive and soon pressure is at the working level, 80 lb per sq. in.

A word with the track steward to check that all is clear and a short warming-up run without load completes the preparations. The locomotive is then moved on to the main line and coupled up to the flat cars which form the train. You and your passengers can now clamber on.

This is where you are asked to turn back to Chapter 3 . . . but instead of gripping the regulator handle with both hands you hold it delicately between finger and thumb. Apart from one person having to do the

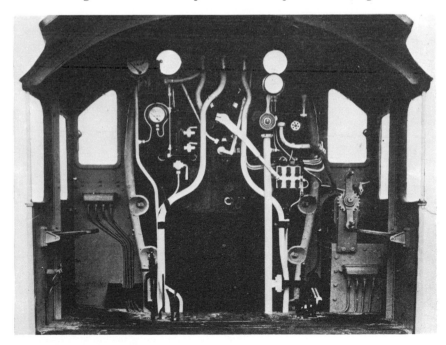

Cab of the same prototype in full-size as a comparison (*British Rail*)

fireman's job as well as the driver's, the main difference on the little one is that, particularly as regards the boiler, time is much condensed. For example, the fire; the few ounces of glowing coals on it can go from white heat to being completely out in a minute or so. On big sister, one is talking of hundred-weights of fire, so there is much more time to think, as well as two people to share the thinking. On the other hand, a full scale railway wreck in $3\frac{1}{2}$ in. gauge is likely to mean a few pieces of sticking-plaster instead of, as in full-size, some one-way trips to the cemetery. A detail difference is that, like *Actaeon* in Chapter 6, the boiler is fed by a mechanical pump, with a hand-operated one in reserve, instead of an injector.

In the master's words . . . 'open the regulator very steady until you feel her pull; then give her just a little more but don't let her slip. Don't notch up yet, but shut the blower-valve and pop a bit on the fire whilst she is puffing hard, a shovelful each side, and one at the back; open the regulator a little more and she will gather speed; now you can notch up, as the blast has pulled the fire through. The water is dropping in the glass, but she is just going to blow off so shut the by-pass and let the lot go into the boiler. This will hold the steam pressure down for a minute or so, but, as the water gets up near the top nut, open the by-pass a little and endeavour to find the setting which keeps the water at that level. The fire will now be fully incandescent, and she will blow off again as the feed is reduced; so open the door and pop on some more coal, same as before. Now you are all set to break the Exeter-Bristol record on a small scale, if you feel like it!' In fact, since the inertia of moving parts on a little locomotive is reduced much more than in proportion to the scale, the wheels can turn much faster than in full size. Scale speeds above not only 100 mph, but 200 mph can be achieved in perfect safety on many tracks, when conditions permit.

Club tracks

Most club tracks are graded flatish like the Exeter-Bristol line but a few are saw tooth like the Cornwall railway. Either way you can enjoy the pleasures and a lot of the sensations of locomotive driving at the cost of a few pence of coal. Even our old friend the rule book is there in scale model form; typically, one-sixteenth full size railways have somewhere around one-sixteenth the number of rules as big brother! Intrinsically, a club means other people and other people mean rules to govern conduct and even the necessity for signalling systems. At the Brighouse club, a semaphore signal was provided (or, at least, was when the writer was a member) which literally 'barred the way' when in the stop position! At other places there is sophisticated automatic multi-aspect signalling in the modern idiom, although with track on stilts, the positioning of the actual signals is totally unrailwaylike. Of course, any failure on your part to maintain steam leading to an unscheduled stop, say, will arouse, in contrast to full-size, derision rather than censure, so there is scope for the trial-and-error method of gaining experience.

The Happy Land of Old
Engines (*H. R. Millar*)

The land where the old engines go

In H. R. Millar's book *Dreamland Express,* he refers to 'the land
where the old engines go'—and can race and run to their hearts'
content. Older readers will remember the days when old steam
engines actually went to the scrap-heap instead of being lovingly
preserved; in this way many famous treasures might seem to have
vanished. Of course in fact they did nothing of the kind—they are
now to be found racing round live steam tracks in all five continents.
Amongst the more enchanting aspects of this little locomotive
business is that the small ones not only exhibit the general
characteristics of steam, but also the particular quirks and qualities
of the particular big sister on which they are modelled.

Of course, not only can one drive such lost treasures as a North-
Western *George V,* a New York Central *Hudson,* a Webb or Vauclain
compound, or a *Fire Fly* single in this way, but one can also drive and
fire might-have-been steam locomotives; not only those from the past
but even from the future—the heroine of Chapter 12 would make an
excellent prototype. Or, perhaps, one might prefer to create a
locomotive to one's very own concept and design, as many have done.

The day having passed most pleasantly in running, in watching
others run and (last but not least) in talking over the most fascinating
of all subjects, it is now necessary to come back to earth with a thud.
Dropping the fire, clearing the ashpan and smoke box, sweeping the
tubes, cleaning down and oiling up is the order of the day. Moreover,

Live steam in America—
4–4–2 on the track of the Los
Angeles Live Steamers
(*Author's collection*)

One can also drive and fire
might-have-been steam
locomotives: 'Curly'
Lawrence's 2–2–2 *Rola*, with
Bobby Jones raising steam
(*Jackie Jones*)

A 5 in. gauge model of the
LNWR *George V* 4–4–0, built
by Geoffrey Cashmore. None
of this type have been
preserved in full size (*G. M.
Cashmore*)

since these clubs are very much co-operatives in the basic sense, there are the chores of cleaning the club rooms, washing-up and sweeping away steam's detritus from the preparation areas.

Yet smaller

Steam is possible in much smaller sizes than these so-called live steam ones, but, since in general the locomotives are not powerful enough to pull normal-sized people, they cannot be driven. In most cases the controls and the fire are set before beginning a run and that is that; the only method of stopping is to grab the hot fiery creature as it goes by.

This was the design principle of Bassett-Lowke's famous locomotive *Enterprise,* which had not even a throttle. There was no water feed system either—you filled the boiler to a prescribed level and the amount of spirit in the lamp tank was designed to be used up before the water-level in the boiler dropped to a dangerous extent. So there was no need for a water gauge and the tender was just an ornament. The length of the spirit-lamp wicks could be set to give a nice steady pace with a modest load on a level continuous track for as long as 45 minutes.

Enterprise was made for $1\frac{1}{4}$ in. gauge (gauge O), a size that is beginning to come down near the limit for a working steam locomotive. It is true that even smaller ones have been made, but they involve a skill which normal people do not have. Indeed, steam locomotives in sizes smaller than gauge O have never been made commercially.

In a size that is a compromise between the $1\frac{1}{4}$ in. and $2\frac{1}{2}$ in. gauges, that is, gauge '1' ($1\frac{3}{4}$ in.), some quite sophisticated control systems have appeared. Between the wars, a Mr V. B. Harrison was one of the pioneers and the principle he adopted was that of a governor, which automatically opened the throttle on up gradients and closed it on down, so keeping the speed of the locomotive constant. By this means the train could be prevented from running away on down gradients, but it was not *driving* in any sense of the word.

An English group from the north of England in 1965 perfected a simple electrical control system for steam locomotives, which involved electric firing as well as control. Messrs Getwood, Mills and Thomson actually ran their line in exacting public conditions on a number of occasions at the annual exhibition of their club (the Manchester Model Railway Society). The precise stops and elaborate shunting were remarkable. The methods used were described in the magazine *Model Railway News* during 1966.

Since then gauge 1 steam locomotives with electrical control but butane gas firing have been offered commercially—at a long price—on the continent of Europe. A notable installation is in Switzerland, at the Basel Model Railway Club, where model steam versions of some of the great steam trains of Europe run (and shunt too) under perfect control.

Such model trains as these do need driving and they do respond to skill, but it is a personal view of the writer that the point at which the driver ceases to be pulled along as he drives is a water-shed. Beyond it, the locomotives might just as well have dummy boilers and be propelled electrically, at one-hundredth the cost and with nine-tenths of the realism. For one thing, the puff has an altogether different and tinnier sound in tiny steam engines, whereas in the live steam sizes it is at least recognizable as belonging to the same family of sounds as that of a full-size locomotive.

As we have seen, all the ways described in these last three chapters of how to get to drive a steam locomotive fall short in one way or another of the real thing. Driving on the live steam sizes involves all the skill and some of the sounds and smells. Long runs on continuous tracks are possible, but their construction on stilts and the ride astride cars are totally un-railway-like.

In the so-called miniature sizes, the driver at least gets to sit on or in the locomotive and in the larger miniatures his head is below the cab roof. The railway itself can be fairly railway-like, with switches, signals and crossings all present and correct.

As regards the full-size pleasure or museum lines, whilst the locomotives are the real thing, the distances and speeds are not. As regards length, none of them in Britain exceeds twenty miles and only four exceed ten. This restrictiveness also applies in America with only very few exceptions. Speeds—without any exceptions—are very low indeed, 25 mph being the maximum.

Nevertheless, in spite of their limitations, all these ways of becoming more or less a steam locomotive driver are being pursued by growing numbers of enthusiastic devotees. At the same time, one must remember that real steam engine driving was done by men who did it day-in and day-out for a living; and any activity, however thrilling in small doses, loses just a little of its attractiveness when it becomes an everyday duty.

STEAM PAST
AND STEAM FUTURE

12

It is amazing to think that twenty short years ago the 15,000-strong steam fleet of British Railways would stretch from London to Crewe, that is, 160 miles buffer-to-buffer. It is even more amazing to think of the people involved—drivers, firemen, fitters and shed-men; a total of 100,000 in one country alone. All men, of course, for steam was (and to a great extent is) a male preserve. Even in China, where female airline pilots and diesel locomotive drivers are unremarkable, steam-engine driving is one of the very few occupations in the People's Republic to be reserved for men. Of this army of steam pensionaires it is strange how many, once steam has got into their blood, find it hard to talk of anything else but the great days.

The words 'hard to imagine' were used in the introduction to describe the possibility of working steam returning. Hard to imagine is right, but not, I think, impossible for the years 2010 *et seq.,* when a large-scale changeover back to coal as a source of energy seems probable. No doubt most railroading will by then be under the wires, ie, electric, but it might just be that economics could dictate the use of steam for such duties as coal leading trips, wiring trains (which have to run when electricity is switched off) or longer runs on lines with insufficient traffic to justify electrification. (Of course, electrification would be justified much more widely in such circumstances, because much more traffic than now would move on rail rather than road.) One such secondary line runs along the coast of Cardigan Bay, in sight of where this is being written.

Forty years on
Imagine you and I meeting in my study on a May morning forty years on, having made the journey there by time machine . . . is that a police 'phone box on the lawn? The unchanging Welsh hills are all around but as railway fanatics we are first of all eager to find out what has happened to the trains. The battery car in the garage shows 30 km 'available range' on the instrument board display and in a moment we are zooming along the road to Penrhyndeudraeth station at its maximum speed of 35 km per hour. As we negotiate the Festiniog Railway level crossing it seems clear that the line's powers of sur-

137

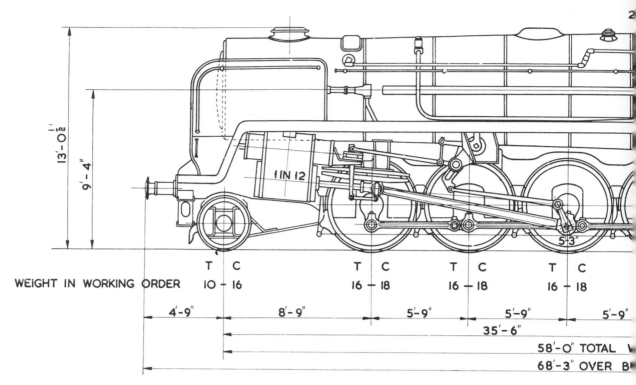

WEIGHT IN WORKING ORDER

	T	C		T	C		T	C		T	C
	10	16		16	18		16	18		16	18

13'-0½"
9'-4"
1 IN 12
5'3"
4'-9"   8'-9"   5'-9"   5'-9"   5'-9"
35'-6"
58'-0" TOTAL
68'-3" OVER B

29 *Moel Siabod*—diagram of the locomotive showing principal weights and dimensions (*Railway Gazette International*)

Boiler barrel diameter (outside)
5 ft 9 in. increasing to 6 ft 5½ in.
Firebox (outside) 7 ft 0 in. long × 7 ft 9 in. to 7 ft 4 in. wide

Tubes
40 large 5½ in. O.D. × 7 S.W.G.
136 small 2⅛ in. O.D. × 11 S.W.G.
Superheater elements—1⅜ in. O.D. × 10 S.W.G.
Length between tubeplates 17 ft 0 in.
Heating surfaces:
Tubes 2264 sq ft
 Firebox 210 sq ft

Total evaporative 2474 sq ft
 Superheater 718 sq ft
Total 3192 sq ft
Grate area 42 sq ft
Cylinders (two) 19½ in. × 28 in.
Tractive effort 35912 lbs
Adhesion factor 4.22
Brake % engine and tender 69.2%
(with trailing truck braked)
Brake load on engine and tender

vival are likely to take it the remaining eighteen years into its third century. A little regenerative braking down the hill into the town gives a small positive urge to the range reading, but even so this little 6 km journey has used a by no means negligible fraction of the electricity stored in our large battery. To go much further we have to take the train . . . but here's the BR station, much as I remember it, except that the signalling and the passing loop have been restored. And in the loop stands a steam-hauled freight. The locomotive is a medium sized 2–8–2 (see Fig 29), very obviously a direct descendant of the BR standard designs of the 1950s. The only obvious external changes are electric lights, an air-pump and (unkindly) a wholly untypical cleanliness.

The driver invites us up—yes, he told us, he's been with steam for

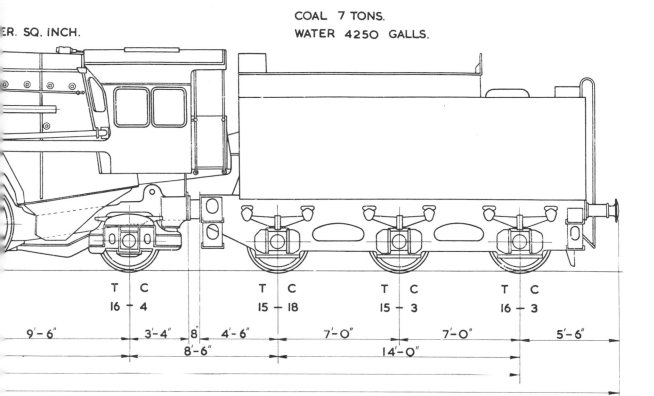

COAL 7 TONS.
WATER 4250 GALLS.

ER. SQ. INCH.

	T	C			T	C		T	C		T	C	
	16	4			15	18		15	3		16	3	

9'- 6" 3'- 4" 8" 4'- 6" 7'- 0" 7'- 0" 5'- 6"
8'-6" 14'-0"

92.85 tons
(with trailing truck braked)

Weights	Full	Empty
Engine	94–12	85–15
Tender	47–4	21–4
Total	141–16	106–19

forty years, beginning as a volunteer on the Severn Valley line and staying on full-time when they prospered. He told us how these new locomotives differed from the ones he drove then . . . .

Underfeed stoker

'First, we don't have to fire, there's an underfeed mechanical stoker. Because this locomotive is a 2–8–2 and not a 2–8–0 or 4–6–0 the firebox is big enough and we can burn 'run-of-the-mine' mechanically dug coal, full of dust and such-like—all there is nowadays. It also leaves behind amounts of ash that would choke one of the museum pieces on the SVR in no time. Most of the air needed comes in above the fire and so we pull very little small coal through into the smokebox when working hard. There's a big hopper ash-pan and we just give the grate a rock from time to time to clean the fire. One thing the designers were forced to do was to make electrics, etc, which can stand up on a steam loco, even in the firebox where conditions are like those on Venus. My mate—they call him 'combustion manager' now—has a video console here in the cab. It's his job always to have steam for me at the specified temperature and pressure and to use the minimum coal in doing so. There's a bonus for this, and if he does well he takes home more than me. He'd also come under heavy fire from the environment people if he allowed black smoke to emerge from the chimney—of course, this is wasteful too but, as well as losing his bonus, he might have to anwer to court. One other job he has is water

Late twentieth-century
steam power: a line of new
2–8–2s outside the works at
Tangshan, China in June
1976 (*D. Scudamore*)

treatment, as consistent application extends boiler life five-fold. The old firm—by this I mean twentieth century BR—could never do it, although they knew how.

'Another thing that was a revolution when we came back into steam was maintenance—the old BR didn't build some bad steamers but the facilities for maintenance were horrible. Most running sheds had most of the roof missing and the tools and equipment were of indescribable crudity—it was really amazing that those old lads did anything, let alone do it well. Nowadays a loco shed has hospital-like cleanliness and proper equipment for white-coated locomotive surgeons to do their operations. Well OK, perhaps I do exaggerate a little, but not much. Another thing that helps is that we just have this one type of locomotive round here.

'Of course, steam is only on a very small scale, the wires now run all along the north coast to Holyhead and down the border from Chester to Shrewsbury and via Hereford to South Wales. Local work and

shunting are electric battery jobs, which leaves through freight and passenger as steam. These little Mikados—that's the traditional name for 2–8–2s—are used on both—in fact one will be along with the Cambrian Coast Express in a minute or two.'

Scientific fireman

The fireman said . . . 'it is strange to think that this job was once done by people who had never heard of the laws of chemistry and physics—practical experience is also important but that on its own is a recipe for disaster. Our firing system here just crept into use in the old days, on a little coal-hauling railway—actually the southernmost in the world—in far way Patagonia, down by Cape Horn. Oddly enough it was not a great distance from that long-lost Welsh colony in that remote part of South America. Again the old BR people knew all about it but the idea was perfected too late, they'd already decided to adopt diesel-engined power. Only some small shunters used by the

British Rail's last steam
locomotive 2–10–0 *Evening
Star* built in 1960 (*British
Rail*)

Coal Board were converted. The idea is that the coal is treated a little
like it is in a gas works, ie, heated to give off gas, rather than being
burnt as in a fire-place. More a chemical reaction than a furnace, if you
like. As well as the advantages my mate has mentioned, you don't get
clinker forming and it's also as good as oil-firing where spark-
throwing and setting fire to woodlands are concerned.

'My training in chemistry also comes in handy in the fight for
clean boilers. Anyone who has boiled a kettle knows how scale
accumulates. What perhaps they don't know is how much heat is
wasted if the water is insulated from the heat source by a layer of
scale—also how much damage this does to the metal plates of the
boiler. In fact, scaled-up boilers are quickly ruined. Equipment on
this locomotive enables me to dose the water in the tank, according to
the acidity or alkalinity of the water in the boiler. This I can test for
on the job without difficulty by drawing a specimen into the test
apparatus, pressing this button and getting a read-out on the console.
The actual solids which, because of the chemicals, accumulate in
suspension instead of as scale inside the boiler, can be blown out of
the boiler by that big valve there, connected to the lowest water
space. I'll just try it, although the water in this particular area is as
pure as any you find . . . .'

Whooosh . . . for a few seconds a great cascade of boiling water
spurts from the side of the boiler with a loud rumbling sound.

Moel Siabod and Moel Tryfan
The Cambrian Coast Express—Pwllheli to London, through coaches
to Cardiff via Shrewsbury—comes rolling down the hill into the
station, a nice polished green engine called *Moel Tryfan* at the
head—all these little 2–8–2s in Wales are apparently named after
Welsh mountains. Strange how these old customs have not died out.

92220

'Now we'll get the road', the driver says and we accordingly descend. In no time the signal displays green and his *Moel Siabod* is sure-footedly moving out on to the single line for the short steep climb to Minffordd.

Whilst the BR standard locomotives were generally excellent, those with pony trucks at the rear suffered a certain lack of surefootedness, ie, a liability to slipping, from not having what is called 'compensated springing'. This 2–8–2 reincarnation, like *Forward* and most of the rest of the world's steam locomotives, can be seen to have this connection between the springing of adjacent wheels which prevents the pony truck stealing adhesive weight from the driving wheels at critical moments, generally due to small track irregularities.

Remembering our experiences on *5428,* it was a pleasure to see mechanical stoking in operation. Conventional mechanical stokers, as has been mentioned, fed coal on to a plate at the back of the firebox, whence it was distributed by steam jets. A problem is that much of the coal—the small bits, anyway—were swept straight down the tubes without ever falling onto the firebed. The waste of partially burnt coal amounted to as much as 10%. This so-called 'underfeed' stoker feeds into the firebed proper.

As this fine locomotive, elegant, simple, convenient to handle and master of its job, pleases us with its fine beat climbing the hill, it is time to leave this unlikely vision of a future whose reality, perhaps fortunately, is veiled from us. The situation described is one where the cost of oil and petrol is many times that of coal and accordingly a diesel or petrol car is as much out of the question for the ordinary citizen as a helicopter is now. It also postulates that powerful batteries, like the sodium-sulphur one, on which work is now being done, will remain laboratory toys and that the inconvenience and

143

possibly the danger of using coal-burning steam cars or producer-gas internal-combustion ones will have kept them as uncommon in 2018 as they always have been in the past.

In such circumstances BR might well climb back from the present mileage of 11,000 towards the 19,000 or so it had when formed in 1948. Electrification might cover as much as half the mileage, on which 90% of the traffic would run. The sparse long-distance traffic on the remainder would be steam hauled by a fleet of some 500 medium-sized steam locomotives of one straightforward type.

Perhaps it is not too much to hope that the rarest and most valuable of qualities, common-sense, would prevail and that design and development would begin where it left off *circa* 1955. In his excellent book *Locomotive Panorama* (Ian Allan, 1966; vols i and ii currently available in paper-back), the steam locomotive design chief of British Rail, Mr E. S. Cox, describes how matters then stood. The foregoing description of 2–8–2s *Moel Tryfan* and *Moel Siabod* assumes that a Chief Officer (Steam Design) would adopt as a basis the BR designs of 1951–5. In fact, the boiler of the class 6 4–6–2 on the chassis of the might-have-been-and-nearly-was class 8 2–8–2 would come out very like these Mountain class 2–8–2s. The very successful class 9 2–10–0 could not be repeated, because of some features of modern high-speed permanent way. The things added, such as compensated springing, a water-treatment system that brought results and 'Patagonian' firing were all steps that might very easily have come had steam continued a few years longer. A little more instrumentation and some elementary physics and chemistry for the man in charge of combustion are my own ideas; easy and even essential in the future when instituting a new tradition but impossible in the past when it was a question of grafting it on to an old one.

Traditions of enginemanship
This is not to say that the old traditions of enginemanship were bad; on the contrary, their excellence was legendary. As I have tried to show in this book, the attraction of steam owes a great deal to the dedication, skill and hard work it exacts from those who handle it. In this respect it was a little like mountaineering, sailing or gliding; difficult, slightly hazardous and often uncomfortable but tremendously rewarding. If in this account of how to do it and how to get to do it I have conveyed to you a fraction of steam's magnetism, then all the effort of writing it down will have been a thousand times worth while.

APPENDIX : LIVE STEAM CLUBS

Listed below are more than 200 known clubs in English speaking parts of the world which cater for the building and driving of steam locomotives. Where known, the location and length of their tracks are given. Contact with the club is best made via its secretary; but secretaries tend to change at fairly frequent intervals, therefore, if you cannot locate a local club from the information given, write—except in the case of Great Britain—to the regional secretary of the Brotherhood of Live Steamers, as given below. In the tradition of the founder of the movement, 'return carriage', in the form of a stamped addressed envelope or international reply coupon, should accompany the query. For Great Britain and North America respectively, the magazines *Model Engineer* (PO Box 35, Hemel Hempstead, Herts, HP1 1EE) and *Live Steam* (PO Box 581, Traverse City, Michigan 49684), will put people in touch with club secretaries, especially if they are subscribers.

THE BROTHERHOOD OF LIVE STEAMERS
Regional Secretaries:
AUSTRALIA   R. V. Wood, PO Box 25, Laurieton, NSW 2443
CANADA   J. R. Kerr, 65 Lanark St., Winnipeg, Manitoba R3N1K8
USA (PACIFIC COAST REGION)   Dwight Durkee, Jr., PO Box 681, Santa Cruz, California 95061
USA (MID WEST REGION)   A. F. Barr, RFD2, Harrisburg, Arkansas 72432
USA (EAST COAST REGION)   B. W. Barnfather, 3 Fleetwood Drive, Sandy Hook, Connecticut 06482

Except for the Great Britain list, the name of the club is given first. Each club also has a title, eg, the entry 'South Coast' refers to the *South Coast Model Engineering Society* and is typical of many of the titles used. The entry 'Western Districts' refers to the *Western Districts Live Steamers* and that title is also typical of many, particularly in the USA.

AUSTRALIA
ADELAIDE, Railway Park, Regency Road, Prospect, Adelaide, S. Australia
BLUE MOUNTAIN, Glenbrook, New South Wales
CASTLEDARE, Castledare, W. Australia
HOBART, Hobart, Tasmania
ILLAWARRA, Woolongong, New South Wales
LAKE MACQUARIE, Edgeworth, New South Wales
QUEENSLAND, Strathpine, Brisbane, Queensland
SOUTH AUSTRALIAN, Millswood, Adelaide, South Australia
SOUTH COAST, The Aerodrome, Albion Park, New South Wales
SYDNEY, Dorvall Park, West Ryde, Sydney, New South Wales
TULLAMARINE, Gladstone Park, Broadmeadows, Melbourne, Victoria
WESTERN AUSTRALIA, Claremont, Perth, West Australia
WESTERN DISTRICTS, Fairfield, New South Wales
VICTORIA, Melbourne, Victoria

CANADA
ATLANTIC, Rothesay, New Brunswick (1400 ft)
BRITISH COLUMBIA, Bonsor Recreation Centre, British Columbia (875 ft)
CALGARY, Calgary, Alberta (720 ft)
FRONTENAC, Kingston, Ontario (500 ft)
GOLDEN HORSESHOE, St. Catharine's, Ontario (250 ft)
GOLDEN TRIANGLE, London, Ontario (1500 ft)
MONTREAL, Les Cadres, Quebec (2200 ft)
ONTARIO SUNPARLOUR, Windsor, Ontario (650 ft)
PETERBOROUGH, Peterborough, Ontario (300 ft)
RED RIVER VALLEY, Winnipeg, Manitoba (780 ft)
VANCOUVER ISLAND, Victoria, British Columbia (700 ft)

GREAT BRITAIN
In Britain the name of the club is usually taken from the town in which it is situated, although in a few cases this is not so and the name of the club is given in brackets after the name of the town. The specific location of the track is then followed by its length, where this is known. Not all the clubs shown admit members of the public and enquiries should be made locally first. Many advise details of open days in the magazine *Model Engineer*. The titles vary, but most incorporate the words 'Model' and 'Engineer'.

The North
BARNSLEY, Dodworth Park (900 ft)
BARROW-IN-FURNESS (Furness) Public Park (800 ft)
BLACKBURN, Murdock St. (330 ft)
BLACKPOOL, (Fylde) King George's Playing Fields (885 ft)
BRADFORD, Northcliffe Woods (440 ft)
BRIGHOUSE, Ravensprings Park, Cawcliffe Rd. (880 ft)
CARLISLE, Upperby Park (450 ft)
CHESTER-LE-STREET, Public Park (500 ft)
DARLINGTON, (S. Durham) Hurworth Grange (1500 ft)
DONCASTER, Sandtoft Trolley Museum (320 ft)
HUDDERSFIELD, Highfields
HULL, Goddard Avenue (460 ft)
KEIGHLEY, St. George's Playing Fields (610 ft)
LEEDS, Temple Newsam Park (1070 ft)
LEYLAND, Worden Park (550 ft)
LIVERPOOL, (Merseyside) Calderstone Park, Allerton (400 ft)
MIDDLESBOROUGH, (Tees-side) Albert Park (600 ft)
NEWCASTLE-UPON-TYNE, Town Moor (650 ft)
ROCHDALE, Springfields St. (720 ft)
SALE, Walton Park
SHEFFIELD, by Omega Restaurant, Chelsea Rd. (480 ft)
STOCKPORT, School for the Deaf (530 ft)
SUNDERLAND, Roker Park (600 ft)
TINGLEY, (W. Riding) Blackgates (670 ft)
URMSTON, Abbotsfield Park (500 ft)
WAKEFIELD, Thomas Park
WARRINGTON, Daresbury Hall (370 ft)
WIGAN, Haigh Park (550 ft)
WIRRALL, Royden Park, Frankby (1200 ft)
YORK, Moor Lane, Dringhouses (440 ft)

Midlands and East Anglia
BEDFORD, 'The Rose', Wilstead (1250 ft)
BIRMINGHAM (Lucas Ltd) Moor Lane, Willon (1040 ft)
BIRMINGHAM, Ilshaw Heath, nr. Solihull (1040 ft)
CAMBRIDGE, Fulbrook Road (750 ft)

CANNOCK CHASE, Cannock Park (800 ft)
CHESTERFIELD, Frank Merifield School (633 ft)
CLEETHORPES, Findus Sports Club, Hewitts Circus
COALVILLE (N. W. Leicestershire), Miner's Welfare Centre
COLESHILL, (Sutton Coldfield) Lea Marston (480 ft)
COLCHESTER, Straight Road, Lexden (480 ft)
CREWE, Beech Drive, Wistaston Green (500 ft)
DERBY, Dr Barnardo's Homes (470 ft)
KING'S LYNN, The Walks Park (712 ft)
KINVER, (West Midlands) (1300 ft)
LEICESTER, Abbey Park (660 ft)
LINCOLN, Boultham Park (510 ft)
MILTON KEYNES, Cosgrave Park
NEWCASTLE-UNDER-LYME, (N. Staffs) Brampton Park (840 ft)
NORTHAMPTON, Delapre Park (830 ft)
NORWICH, Eaton Park (830 ft)
NOTTINGHAM, Valley Rd. (1136 ft)
PETERBOROUGH, Lincoln Road
RUGBY, Hillmorton Rd. (450 ft)
STAFFORD, Staffordshire Agricultural Showground
TELFORD, (Phoenix)
WILLASTON, (S. Cheshire), Horseshoe Hotel (5000 ft)

Home Counties

AYLESBURY, Bifurcated Rivet Co's Sports Ground (420 ft)
BRACKNELL, Jocks Lane (1000 ft)
BRENTWOOD, Woodway, Shenfield (440 ft)
CHELMSFORD, Waterhouse Lane (1000 ft)
CHINGFORD, Ridgeway Park (1200 ft)
COLNEY HEATH, (N. London) Tyttenshanger Park (2393 ft)
ERITH, Track at Dartford
HARLINGTON, High Street (1100 ft)
HARROW, BR Sports Ground, Headstone Lane (550 ft)
HARROW & WEMBLEY, Roxbourne Park
HATFIELD, (360 ft)
HIGH WYCOMBE, The Rye
HITCHIN, Grove Road (360 ft)
ICKENHAM, 'Coach and Horses' (330 ft)
MALDEN, Claygate Lane, Thames Ditton (1650 ft)
NORTHOLT, Community Centre, Ealing Road (750 ft)
QUAINTON ROAD, (Vale of Aylesbury), Steam Centre
ROMFORD, Ardleigh Ho., Hornchurch (850 ft)
READING, Prospect Park (1000 ft)
SUTTON, Chatham Close, Woodstock Rise (530 ft)
WELLING, Russell Park, Bexleyheath (480 ft)
WILLESDEN, Roundwood Park (300 ft)

The West and South

ANDOVER, Redrice (730 ft)
BASINGSTOKE, Viables Farm
BOURNEMOUTH, King's Park
BRIGHTON, Hove Park (338 ft)
BRISTOL, Ashton Park (1646 ft)
CANTERBURY, Sturry
CHELTENHAM, Hatherley Lane (675 ft)
CHICHESTER, Coe's Garage, Bognor Road (560 ft)
CRAWLEY, Goff's Park (1320 ft)
DEVIZES, Townsend, Great Cheverill (380 ft)
EXETER, Princess Elizabeth Social Club
GUILDFORD, Stoke Park (666 ft)

HASTINGS, Essenden Road (580 ft)
HAYWARDS HEATH, (Sussex) Beechurst (2200 ft)
HEREFORD, Bulmer's Steam Centre
ISLE OF WIGHT, Broadfields, Cowes (650 ft)
MAIDSTONE, Rote Park (2000 ft)
NEW ROMNEY, (Romney Marsh) Rolfe Lane (350 ft)
NEWTON ABBOT, Penn Inn Park (360 ft)
PAIGNTON, (Torbay)
PERRANPORTH, Callestick
PLYMOUTH, Crabtree Close
POLEGATE, Martello Beach
PORTSMOUTH, Brandsbury Park (700 ft)
RAMSGATE, Ellington Park (500 ft)
SOUTHAMPTON, Bitterne Park (1080 ft)
TIVERTON, Blundell's School (530 ft)
TONBRIDGE, Castle Hill Gardens
WESTBURY, The Youth Centre
WESTON-SUPER-MARE, New Road, Huntspill (530 ft)
WOODSTOCK (Witney), Blenheim Park (1320 ft)

Northern Ireland
BELFAST, Ulster Transport Museum

Scotland
EDDLESTON, (Edinburgh), Old Railway Station (900 ft)
GLASGOW
KIRKINTILLOCH, Woodhead Park (480 ft)

Wales
CARDIFF, Highfields Road, Whitchurch (700 ft)
LLANDUDNO, Ysgol Gogarth (520 ft)
NEWPORT, (St. Mellons) St. Julien's Glebe Lands (3040 ft)
SWANSEA, Derwen Fawr, Sketty (600 ft)
SWANSEA, Heol-y-Gorf, Cwmbwra (600 ft)
WREXHAM, Pant-yr-Ochain Farm, Gresford (800 ft)

NEW ZEALAND
CANTERBURY, Christchurch
HUTT VALLEY, Petone, Wellington
NELSON, Tahuna Beach, Nelson
OTAGO, Dunedin

SOUTHERN AFRICA
PORT ELIZABETH, Lundt Park, Port Elizabeth, S. Africa
RAND, Milner Park, Johannesburg, S. Africa
SALISBURY, Rainhill Park, Salisbury, Zimbabwe

Also at BLOEMFONTEIN, BULAWAYO, CAPE TOWN, DURBAN, EAST LONDON, PIETERMARITZBURG, PRETORIA and UPINGTON

UNITED STATES
Pacific Coast Region
ALASKA, State Fair Grounds, Palmer Anchorage (1400 ft)
ANTELOPE VALLEY, Lancaster & Quartz Hill, California (780 ft)
CHULA VISTA, Rohr Park, Chula Vista, California (2500 ft)
COLORADO, Black Forest, Colorado (1280 ft)
GOLDEN GATE, Tilden Park, Berkeley, California (5250 ft)
GOLETA VALLEY, Santa Barbara, California (8000 ft)
INLAND EMPIRE, Couer d'Alene & Lewiston, Idaho (1250 ft)
JOSHUA TREE & SOUTHERN, Joshua Tree, California (860 ft)
LONG BEACH, El Dorado Park, Long Beach, California
LOS ANGELES, Los Angeles, California (5000 ft)
PACIFIC NORTH WEST, Shady Dell, Molalla, Oregon (5500 ft)
RIVERSIDE, Hunter Park, Riverside, California (8691 ft)
SACRAMENTO VALLEY, Rancho Cordova, Community Park, Sacramento California (2500 ft)
SOUTHERN CALIFORNIA, Lowita, California
WESTERN WASHINGTON, Shelton, Washington (3100 ft)

Mid-West Region
CENTRAL ILLINOIS, Mattoon, Illinois (400 ft)
CINDER SNIFFERS, Dover, Indiana (1575 ft)
GEORGIA, Smyrna & Jackson, Georgia (580 ft)
HOUSTON, Texas (440 ft)
ILLINOIS, Lamont, Illinois(4000 ft)
INDIANA, Pendleton, Indiana (500 ft)
IOWA, Marion, Iowa (925 ft)
KANSAS CITY, Agricultural Hall of Fame, Bonner Springs, Kansas
LAPORTE COUNTY HISTORICAL STEAM SOCIETY, Heston, Indiana
MARICOPA, Scottsdale, Arizona (2400 ft)
MID SOUTH, Maury County Park, Columbia, Tennessee (3600 ft)
MILWAUKEE, Menominee Falls, Wisconsin (2500 ft)
MINNESOTA, Rochester & Lake City, Minnesota (5280 ft)
OMAHA AREA, Papillion, Nebraska (2000 ft)
SAN ANTONIO, Texas (1000 ft)
ST CROIX, Hudson, Wisconsin (1000 ft)
ST LOUIS, Missouri (800 ft)
SOUTH WESTERN, Anneta, Texas
WABASH, FRISCO & PACIFIC, Glencoe, Missouri (5600 ft)

East Coast Region
CHESAPEAKE & ALLEGHENY, Age of Steam Museum, Yorklyn, Delaware (1500 ft)
DELAWARE, Wilmington, Delaware (2000 ft)
FINGER LAKES, Marengo, New York State (1100 ft)
FLORIDA, Maitland 6 Homestead, Florida (5900 ft)
LAKE SHORE, Mentor, Ohio (1345 ft)
LONG ISLAND, South Haven, New York (2400 ft)
NEW JERSEY, Liberty Corners, New Jersey (2500 ft)
NIAGARA FRONTIER, West Seneca, New York State (750 ft)
NORTH EASTERN OHIO, Copley, Ohio (2300 ft)
PENNSYLVANIA, Rahns, Pennsylvania (1800 ft)
PENSACOLA, Flonde (500 ft)
PIONEER VALLEY, Southwick, Massachusetts (5600 ft)
SOUTH JERSEY, Haddon Heights, New Jersey (400 ft)
WAUSHAKUM, Holliston, Massachusetts (1100 ft)
WEST PENN, Beaver County, Pittsburgh, Pennsylvania (720 ft)

BIBLIOGRAPHY

Cecil J. Allen, *Locomotive Practice and Performance in the Twentieth Century,* Heffer, 1955

W. G. Chapman, *The King of Railway Locomotives,* Great Western Railway, 1928

E. S. Cox, *Locomotive Panorama,* (two volumes), Ian Allan, 1964

R. H. N. Hardy, *Steam in the Blood,* Ian Allan, 1969

J. T. Hodgson and C. S. Lake, *Locomotive Management,* St. Margaret's Technical Press, (8th edition) 1942

J. B. Hollingsworth, *Steam for the Seventies,* New English Library, 1971

J. B. Hollingsworth, J. B. Snell and P. B. Whitehouse, *Steam for Pleasure,* Routledge and Kegan Paul, 1978

'LBSC', *Shops, Shed and Road,* Model and Aeronautical Press, 1960

E. T. McDermot, *History of the Great Western Railway,* (two volumes), Great Western Railway, 1927

N. McKillop, *Ace Enginemen,* Nelson, 1963

H. R. Millar, *Dreamland Express,* Oxford University Press, 1927

P. W. B. Semmens, *Engineman Extraordinary,* Ian Allan, 1962

Peter Smith, *Footplate over the Mendips,* Oxford Publishing Company, 1978

J. W. Street, *I Drove the Cheltenham Flyer,* Nicholson and Watson, 1951

H. E. White, *Maintenance and Management of Small Locomotives,* Percival Marshall, 1955

—*Manual for Steam Locomotive Enginemen,* British Railways, 1960

—*Rule Book,* British Railways, 1950

—*Rules and Regulations of the Transportation Department,* Southern Pacific Railroad, 1976

INDEX

STOP

Arms raised and low-
ered as shown for as
fast a stop as desired.